The Church Doctor

JOHN NEWELL

WESTBOW°
PRESS
A DIVISION OF THOMAS NELSON
& ZONDERVAN

WestBow Press books may be ordered through booksellers or by contacting:

WestBow Press
A Division of Thomas Nelson & Zondervan
1663 Liberty Drive
Bloomington, IN 47403
www.westbowpress.com
1 (866) 928-1240

ISBN: 978-1-4908-6561-4 (sc)
ISBN: 978-1-4908-6562-1 (e)

Library of Congress Control Number: 2015900165

Printed in the United States of America.

WestBow Press rev. date: 3/17/2015

Three Basic Characteristics of "Do-nothing" congregations

1. IGNORANT:

   You know not the word of God for yourselves

2. FEARFUL:

   You know not what it means to be of good courage

3. APATHETIC:

   You do not watch for the hour of the thief

Contents

Three Basic Characteristics of "Do-nothing"
congregations v
The Author xi
The Ten Commandments xiii

SECTION 1

Commonly Asked Questions 2

Chapter 1   Who is God? 5
    Laws 7
    The church and the law 9
    Exodus 20:1-17 The Ten Commandments Explained 11
    The Law: Simplification I 13
    The Law: Simplification II 15
    The Law: Simplification III 15

Chapter 2   The First and Great Commandment 16
    1. Thou shalt have no other Gods before God. 17
    2. Thou shalt not make unto thee any graven
        image, or any likeness of anything that is in
        heaven above, or that is in the earth beneath,
        nor that is in the water, under the earth. 18

3. Thou shalt not take the name of the Lord thy
   God in vain. 18

4. Remember the Sabbath day, to keep it holy. 19

5. Honor thy father and thy mother: that thy days
   may be long upon the land which the Lord thy
   God giveth thee.. 20

Chapter 3   The Second and Great Commandment..... 21

   Spiritual and physical death... 25

   Church and home adultery 27

   Church and social stealing.. 29

   Witnessing and Lying 32

   The mindset of covetousness 33

SECTION 2

The Christian Family 38

Chapter 4   To the Church 41

   Faith 43

   Faith, Level One 45

   Faith Level 2 48

   Faith Level 3 50

   Faith Level 4 51

Chapter 5   Ships of Zion... 53

   Wor-ship 54

   Christian Steward-ship 55

   Disciple-ship.. 60

   Christian Fellow-ship... 62

SECTION 3

What Can Christians Do? 66

Chapter 6   Selecting Godly leadership......................... 69
Identifying the ungodly Leaders 71
Statements that misrepresent the Word of God 74
The Golden Calf: The Most Dangerous Leader...............76

SECTION 4

Words.. 80

Chapter 7   Spiritual Warfare 81
Types of spiritual warfare... 84
The Battlefield 87
The Christian Soldier 88
The Congregation: You are the salt of the earth 89

Chapter 8   Weapons of Christian warfare 96
The Adversary 97
Fiery Dots of the Devil... 98

Chapter 9   The Word 102
God is the ultimate authority in the Church.................102

SECTION 5

Chapter 10   Church Structure & Constitution.............106
CHURCH STRUCTURE...108
Congregational Care Committee...................................108
Base Rules of Unity 110
Salvation Coordinator...112
Church Projects...113

The Author

Mr. John Newell was born in the forties in Laurel, Mississippi to the Reverend Cecil and Josephine Newell. He is the third oldest child in a family of nine siblings, which consist of five boys and four girls. Newell was reared in an atmosphere of ministry as his father served as a Baptist minister.

Newell has several uncles who served as Baptist deacons just as his grandfather did.

Joining the Missionary Baptist Church at the age of seven, Newell has not been away from the church for more than ten months over all of the many years of serving in the Church. John served as a trainee Sunday school teacher in the church which he was baptized at the age of 12 years old.

In his lifetime, Newell has been a member of five different congregations where he served and chaired on most standard church committees. During that time, he has served in God's ministries under approximately ten pastors.

Relocating to Nashville, where he has been for many years, Newell served as a deacon in the same congregation for over 23 years.

Newell made a living in the area of communication for thirty years. He also organized and operated four different businesses following his service in the United States Army where he received an honorable discharge.

John Newell currently resides in Nashville, Tennessee with his wife of forty years. Their union provided them with two children, one son and one daughter, who now have children of their own.

As Newell has travelled to many countries and attended four different colleges and universities, he always found the area of psychology to be most interesting. "Man's fight to get right with Him has always fascinated me," he said. "I have found that the Holy Bible and God's plan of salvation is the best approach to 'get right' with himself and his environment."

The Ten Commandments

The Ten Commandments are our stairway to heaven
which is a safe haven for those who
wish to shew the devil.
It is the light upon the hill shining bright for all to see,
the good, the bad, the wrong,
the right and the souls of men
that contain the light.
It is the breath of life for the church of Christ.
It is the heartbeat of a loving wife
that contains the wishes of her Christ.
It is a tool for a loving mother to curve
the action of a wayward son —
a means by which we all may escape the devil's charm.
It is a tool that an almighty God placed beneath the sun
for the children of God, to Him may come.

By John W. Newell

SECTION 1

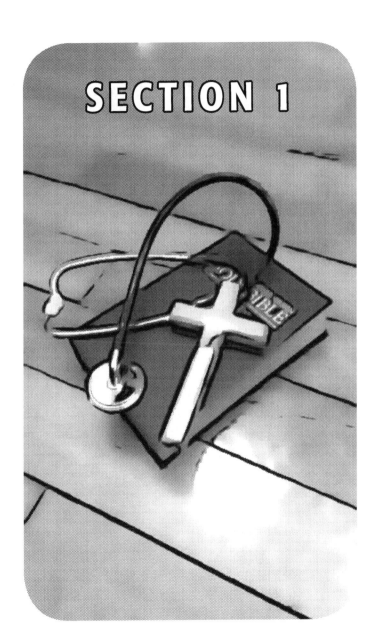

Commonly Asked Questions

Do good people go to hell for not confessing God?
Keeping in mind that only God is good, Christians strive
for perfection simply because they fall short of all that God
would have them to do. A so-called good man has satisfied
the first requirement for salvation. He has repented.
Repentance is having a godly sorrow for sin, a turning
away from wrong doing. God is spirit. The spirit of God is
a spirit of truth, righteousness and justice. Any man that
lives his life with a spirit of truth, righteousness and justice
is in God and God is in him. This man's life is a confession
more so than those who confess with their mouth.

**What do we do when the Bible is not clear about the
actions that should be taken?** The first thing to do is study
the word. Secondly, make sure that what is done does not
violate the Ten Commandments. Thirdly, make sure that
actions support the attributes of God. Fourth, apply the
Golden Rule. Last, but not least, pray for insight.

Why does God allow hardship? A more appropriate
question is "Why does man allow hardship?" Genesis 1:28
God created man in His own image and placed him on
earth a little lower than the angels in heaven. God gave
man all that he needed to survive. Man did not have the
need to distinguish between what is good and what is not,

what is wise and what is not. Genesis 3:20 man's choice against the will of God to be able to distinguish between good and evil represented the death of man as God created. Man is equipped with only the capacity of success. Man moved from a life of success to a life of a capable success for now he has the ability to be good or evil. Evil sources or selfish choices of man cause starvation. Evil choices or selfish choices cause war. Evil choices or selfish choices cause disease. God has a free will philosophy that respects man's right of choice. With this same free will philosophy God gives all men the choice to become born again, a child of God that works to eliminate the hardship of this world.

Should homosexuality be supported by church and country? In order to place this question in content, let us first ask, "What should the church support or not support?" The Church should support all things that are sacred according to the Church. According to the Church, it is sacred, if it is of God. Nothing is sacred apart from God. God is holy. The Bible is sacred because it has the word of God in it. Jesus Christ is sacred because He is the son of God. Mary is sacred because she represents the means by which the son arrived on earth. The cross is sacred because it represents the completion of the will of God. The sacraments are actions or things by which God's grace is communicated. The Holy Scripture, Genesis 2:24, a man shall leave his father and his mother and shall cleave unto his wife and they shall be one flesh. Genesis 2:28 be fruitful and multiply. This is the composition of the sacred family. This is the family composition that is capable of carrying out the will of God. Any other family composition is apart from God. This is the only biological family that the church or those of God can approve. Any other family composition attempts to change or alter the word, as well as the wisdom of God.

Why should I believe in a God I cannot see? The first question is, "Do you believe in men you cannot see?" God is spirit and man was created in the image of God. The spirit of man is in the body. The spirit of God is life eternal. The life and the spirit are one. The spirit maintains the body. Our eyes cannot perceive the spirit of man or God. The word of God tells us that the spirit of God is good. The Bible tells us that after the fall of man, he had the will to choose the good spirit of God or the evil spirit of Satan. Man can only perceive man and God with his mind. Man who desires to see God with his eyes complicates God's purpose. The second question is, "What body may God select that may enhance the unity of a divided world?"

CHAPTER 1

Who is God?

The first and foremost important thing that any church member or church leaders should know is "Who God is." Even though we cannot fully see God, we still can know Him. We've come to know Him through a personal relationship of faith and what the Bible teaches about Him. Seeing the god they serve is a common requirement of those who serve other gods. This also sets those who serve God apart from those who do not. Other gods have three common qualities. They have physical images of attraction; they lack or are not capable of moral qualities and are universally destructive. A common definition of a god may be defined as someone or something that is put before the morality of God.

The morality of God may be perceived in the Ten Commandments. Money or gold, as many other things, become man's god when the love for these things are placed before the love of God. Exodus 20:3-4 God said, Thou shall not have any other gods before me and that he is a jealous

God. For an individual or a church to experience a true relationship with God, they must know that the God they served is the creator and sustainer of the universe. The three most common gods that are served before the almighty God today are man, wealth and one or two of man's transgressed behaviors. God is spirit. He must be worshipped in spirit and in truth. Gen. 1: 27 Man was created in the image of God by God. The fall of man gave man the opportunity to maintain or refrain from that image. This makes God man's heavenly father. This makes God worthy of the 5th commandment and man ward of the first promise. A physical image of God may be perceived in the face of those who best keep the commandments of God. When man accepted the word of God, God is in him and he is in God.

Attributes of God are visible in those who are full of the Holy Ghost. The full revelation of God is in Jesus, the Christ. Look to Christ for direction and not man. When we worship man, we worship that man's god, whether it is money, silver, gold, sex, bearing false witness or misusing God or fellow man. God may be known in terms of his natural attributes. Attributes are inherited characteristics of personalities or beings. There are natural attributes of God: God is spirit (John 4:24); God has no physical or measurable form. God is changeless (Heb. 1:12) He does not change; He need not change, for He is perfect. God is all powerful (Gen. 18:1) "Impossible" is not in God's vocabulary. God is everywhere. He is the God of all the earth, (Gen. 18:25) God is eternal; Eternity refers to God's relation to time. 2 Peter 3:8; Rev. 1:8 The past, present and future are known equally to Him. These natural attributes allows man to know who God is. King David, after contemplating the natural attributes of such a God, stated, "What is man that God would be mindful of man."

But after we ponder the moral attributes of this God, those attributes that keep all natural powers in perspective, sparks a hope for a world of darkness and to be an example for the world to follow. God is holy. God is separated from or exalted above other things (Is. 6:1-3) God is righteous. Righteousness as applied to God refers to His affirmation of what is right. This is also what He commands of His followers. God is love. Love is the essential, self-giving nature of God. God is truth. All truth, whether natural, physical or religious, is grounded in God. God is wisdom. All wisdom comes from God. Man lacking wisdom may obtain it by trusting in God, 1King, 3-9.

Laws

Laws are a rule of conduct binding on an individual, group or organization. There are two types of laws, secular and non-secular. The difference in secular laws and non-secular laws is that secular laws are laws are not religiously binding. These secular laws may or may not be the same as non-secular laws. Non secular laws are given to us by God.

People also have personal laws. As sure as there is life in your body you are living by a law and it is a law that is controlling your destiny. Many times these laws conflict with each other. The totality of life is composed of laws. We choose to live by 1 John 3: 4. Whosoever commit sin transgresses the law, for sin is the transgression of the law of God. To understand what a religious law is we must come to a clear definition of what religion is.

Religion is the belief in a supernatural power recognized as the creator and ruler of the universe. Religion declares this all wise and knowing, living person as God. Over two thirds of six billion people believe in this God. St John 1:1 tells us that this God has been around since the beginning of time. This means that the difference in a religious law and a non-religious law is that the religious law was written by an all-powerful, all knowing God. This means that these laws have already been tested and approved. These laws were written by a kind and loving creator. John 3:16 says that God so loved the world, that He gave his only begotten son, so we may understand the religious law.

Matthew 5:17- Think, not that I am come to destroy the law or prophets: I am not come to destroy, but to fulfill the law. This says that God's law was workable when He gave them--when He gave His son, and when He gave me life. 1. The other laws change on a daily basis. This may be confusing. 2. Man complicates things. Man's law has a library of rules, regulations and stipulations. God gave ten laws. Pharisees looks God in the face and said, "I don't understand." Jesus said, "Keep the first or second laws and you have kept all ten." 3. God is love. God's laws have love in them. What does love have to do with it? Everything. The ten laws are one and the one law has two significant areas of concern. The one law is concerned with peace on earth. The one law gives man two means of accomplishing this objective.

The first and foremost way is on the love of God. Thus, called the first great commandment. The second way is the love and respect man has for each other, the second great command.

The church and the law

The Church is an assembly of those who believe in the Christ. Christ is the one who was sent by God to teach the word of God. Christ established the church on the principle that those who believe in Him, believes that He, the Christ's life and death represented the will of God for HIs people. When we as a church or individually go contrary to God's will, we sin. God's will is often defined as laws.

God's will for His people may be perceived in many ways. The basic way by which a church may retain God's will, is to retain God's laws as written. This means that a church ministry must maintain an uncompromising position about the laws of God. St. John (1:1 makes no difference in God and His word. When the church accepts the word of God, the church accepts God.

When the church does not accept the laws of God as is, it displays a God which should not be accepted as is. To correct God's law is to correct God. When there is a love for the word of God in the church, the church prospers. Spiritual powers come from God. The word of God and God are one. When a church keeps the word of God as is, they keep their God as well as the spirit of God-as is. For God is spirit. With the arrival of the world and the law comes the presence of the power of the father, the son and the Holy Spirit.

The concept of today's church has come to be conceived as a group of individuals who assemble on a regular basis at a designated place for the purpose of praising God. This concept of the church has the tendency to project the idea that the church's purpose and authority should remain within these boundaries. Along with this concept comes misplaced authority, as well as, misplaced boundaries.

Misplaced authority and misplaced boundaries provide non-Christian leaders with the fantasy that they are and not God, is the ultimate authority. The basic concept of the church is that Christ established one church in which all Christians belong. Christ established one church where all Christians are equally responsible for fighting evil inside, as well as, outside of God's assemblies. The way of the devil is a divider, an ostracizer and a gerrymander--three common practices of an ungodly assembly. The church boundaries surround all life and by the authority Christ invested in the lives of the church, under the direction of God, He gives the church the authority to enhance the kingdom of God, as well as, peace in the world by the acceptance of the responsibility of preaching and teaching God's principle to all nations.

The failure of today's church to take a perfect approach to accomplishing this objective is spear-headed by a poor selection of spiritual leadership. The biblical qualifications for the selection of spiritual leaders are ignored. Many of today's spiritual leaders do not have or display any respect for those who display basic Christian attributes. This failure of today's church to accomplish their objective is compounded by a lack of churches to remove leaders who display a lack of respect for God's laws.

A "good" church does not compromise God's word. A "good" church does not allow a leader to compromise God's word. A "good" church does not allow division at the request of members or leaders.

"Good" church supports in voice and votes those who

are within the boundaries of truth and righteousness. A "good" church understands the support of those who are right, supports Christ. Those who support wrong, supports Satan. A "good" church should expect thriving leaders to have the ability to deal constructively with all members. A "good" church understands that accountability and credibility should be protocol. A "good" church understands that the lack of protocol is the number one source of division. A "good" church understands that accountability and being credible are both signs of good stewardship. A "good" church understands to trust and teach God's law is the responsibility of the church.

Exodus 20:1-17 The Ten Commandments Explained

You have probably heard, "No person is able to live up to the Ten Commandments." To some, this statement voids the need to try to live up to them. Living up to the Ten Commandments is not God's goal for those who believe in Him. It is God's beginning point for all who seek to know and love Him. The Ten Commandments are man's opportunity to see and know who God is and what He is about. To believe in the Ten Commandments do not mean that you have perfected that belief. It means that you will strive to perfect that which you believe. The Ten Commandments are God's oil by which He has provided for man to work the miracles of His kingdom. The Ten Commands are also a tool by which God's followers may discern who possesses the Holy Ghost which is vital for the selection of leaders of the church. It is a device by which God has divided the world into the only division that is acceptable by Him. He divides the world into two parts, good and evil. It brings to reality an invisible God and the invisible word of God. The Ten Commandments is a rule of order that projects and injects means by which all men may enjoy life more abundantly.

Repentance is the ability to believe and see the possibilities in doing things God's way while retaining a godly sorrow for those who don't. This belief inspires trust and faith in God's movement for life liberty and the pursuit of happiness for all people. This is faith level one.

The first five commandments have commands regarding our relationship with our heavenly father whereas the fifth commandment is inclusive of our earthly father. The last five commandment deals with how people are to treat our neighbor.

The first great commandment instructs the children of God how to keep the first five commandments. The second great commandment tells us how we shall treat our fellow man.

No one can explain the Ten Commandments more so than Jesus Christ. The gospel of Christ was centered around the Ten Commandments. One of Christ's chief purposes was to clear up many of the fallacies the Pharisees had about the Ten Commandments. With the Ten Commandments God made a covenant of Himself with a people that would be a treasure unto Him. Exodus 20:5-6-Those who believe in God believe in the Ten Commandments. The Ten Commandments are the words of God. St. John 1:1 says, "Even in the beginning was the word, and the word was with God and the word was God."

Those who believe in God is "God's pot of gold." Who, but a non-believer, would have the audacity to attempt to rob God. Any man, boy or nation who cannot appreciate the Ten Commandments should not be allowed to represent God. The Ten Commandments is a document with an aim of peace and good will for all mankind. Anyone who boldly places pictures on the walls of an adulterer, a thief, a killer, one who bears false witness and alike and will not display the Ten Commandments do not believe in God or His word for the Ten Commandments are the face of God.

The Law: Simplification I

And God spoke all these words saying, "I am the Lord thy God, which have brought thee out of the land of Egypt, out of the house of bondage."

1. Thou shalt have no other gods before me.

2. Thou shalt not make unto thee any graven image, or any likeness of anything that is in heaven above or that is in the earth beneath, or that is in the water under the earth:

    Thou shalt not bow down thyself to them, nor serve them: For I, the Lord thy God, am a jealous God, visiting the iniquity of the fathers upon the children unto the third and fourth generation of them that hate me: And, showing mercy unto thousands of them that love me, and keep my commandments.

3. Thou shalt not take the name of the Lord, thy God, in vain; for the Lord will not hold him guiltless that taketh His name in vain.

4. Remember the Sabbath Day, to keep it holy. Six days shalt thou labor, and do all thy work: But the seventh day is the Sabbath of the Lord thy God; in it thou shalt not do any work, thou nor thy son, nor thy daughter, nor thy manservant, nor their maidservant, nor thy cattle, nor thy stranger that is within thy gates. For in six days the Lord made heaven and earth, the sea and all that is in them and rested on the seventh day, wherefore the Lord blessed the Sabbath day and hallowed it.

5. Honor thy father and thy mother: that thy days may be long upon the land which the Lord thy God giveth thee.

6. Thou shalt not kill.

7. Thou shalt not commit adultery.

8. Thou shalt not steal.

9. Thou shalt not bear falls witness against thy neighbor.

10. Thou shalt not covet thy neighbor's house, shalt not covet thy neighbor's wife, nor his manservant, nor his maidservant, no his ox, nor his ass, nor anything that is thy neighbors.

The Law: Simplification II

The First and Great Commandment

> *Thou shalt love the Lord thy God with all thy heart and with all thy soul and with all thy mind.*

The Second and Great Commandment

> *Thou shalt love thy neighbor as thyself.*

The Law: Simplification III

The Golden Rule St. Matt. 8:12-Therefore, all things, whatsoever ye would that men should do to you, do ye even to them: for this is the law and the prophets. These are the laws that all church members must believe unchanged or unmodified. No man is wise enough to improve what God proclaims.

CHAPTER 2

The First and Great Commandment

Thou shalt love the Lord thy God with all thy heart, and with all thy soul and with all thy mind.

a. Thou shalt have no other Gods before me.

b. Thou shalt not make unto thee any graven image, or any likeness of anything that is in heaven above, or that is in the earth beneath, nor that is in the water, under the earth

c. Thou shalt not take the name of the Lord thy God in vain.

d. Remember the Sabbath day, to keep it holy.

e. Honor thy father and thy mother: that thy days may be long upon the land which the Lord thy God giveth thee.

f. The Lord, our God, will like to remind us that there are other things, other spirits, other forces, that we will encounter during our brief stay on earth. Many of these spirits will appear to be safe and rewarding spirits for us to place our faith and eventually our lives. He would like to remind us that the price we pay to serve these forces are to put them before Him. God's word is God. Any life endeavor that requires us to transgress God's word, places that endeavor above God. If we love God we will keep His commandments. When our love for any graven images exceeds our love for God, that image becomes our director, our guiding light, our God.

1. Thou shalt have no other Gods before God.

b. Man is weak and needs the strength of the spirit of God to be a blessing on earth and to the kingdom of heaven. God's wish for man is that he will serve with Him as the gardener for the world. This work requires man's spirit, man's image, man's wisdom to reflect an understanding of the moral and natural attributes of God. No physical element or transgressed force is capable of cultivating the salvation of the world. God is spirit. We must worship God in the spirit.

2. Thou shalt not make unto thee any graven image, or any likeness of anything that is in heaven above, or that is in the earth beneath, nor that is in the water, under the earth.

c.   The name of the Lord, our God, has come to represent love, truth, righteousness and justice. Because of these moral attributes the name of God has been exalted above all other names. Because man has been able to move from a destructive state to a constructive state, the name of God must be held in high esteem. When we misrepresent the things that He has done and the words that He said, we take the name of the Lord in vain. When we call someone a "fool" for not transgressing God's laws, when the opportunity prevails, we are not only stating that the word of God is vain, but we are also calling God a fool. Another common vain statement is, "If God didn't want me to steal it, he would not have put it in front of me."

3. Thou shalt not take the name of the Lord thy God in vain.

d.   Almighty God created the earth in six days and on the seventh day He rested. On the seventh day God rested from the work of creating the earth and on the seventh day He blessed the seventh day. The seventh day represented the completion of a good work. The seventh day should stand as a monumental reminder of the greatness of our God, as well as, the concern and love He displays for man event to the point of man and His work. This is the first of the two great commandments that do not start with "thou shall not." It took the goodness of God to perform the work of creating the heaven and the earth. It takes goodness of another to participate in the salvation of the world. God reminds us that work should never be placed before the goodness of God and His word.

4. Remember the Sabbath day, to keep it holy.

e.   In an everlasting effort of God to remind man the value of man accepting him and him alone as being His guiding light, the fifth commandment reminds man that God has the same concerns for his children that earthly fathers should have for their children. God desires the blessing and safety for all of His children, the same as an earthy father should. The task of an earthly and our heavenly father is to get their children to understand that prior years of life experiences of a loving father can be wisdom for the mind and light for the feet of the young that heed their word.

5. Honor thy father and thy mother: that thy days may be long upon the land which the Lord thy God giveth thee.

Summary

The first five commandments tell us how we may build a stronger relationship with God. These five commandments warn us of temptation of life that we will face, that our mind, eyes, ears, nose, and skin will support the opinion that life apart from Him can be a worthy life. They tell us that God is spirit and we must worship Him in spirit. His word is spirit for HIs word is Him and we should place them and His word above all things. This is the first and foremost way of obtaining eternal life.

CHAPTER 3

The Second and Great Commandment

Thou shalt love thy neighbor as thyself

- a. Thou shalt not kill.
- b. Thou shalt not commit adultery.
- c. Thou shalt not steal.
- d. Thou shalt not bear false witness against thy neighbor.
- e. Thou shalt not covet thy neighbor's house; thou shalt not covet thy neighbor's wife, nor his manservant, nor his maid servant, nor his ox, nor his ass, nor any thing that is thy neighbor's.

It is not hard to understand an artist that is unhappy when one of his good works is destroyed or made useless. It is understandable when a father grieves at the sight of the physical or spiritual death of a child. Then, I trust that you must understand the compound grief, of the father of father and the artist of artist endure at a single lost child. Can you visualize the love and respect a father, who is able to move mountain and sling stars across the universe must have for that child to endure years of tribulation for that child to come to his senses? The pain he must feel when one of his sons take upon himself to take the life of that son.

No son of God knows the hour of repentance of a brother No son has the right of robbing God of the opportunity for his son to enter the kingdom of God. Only the Lord is able to give life. Only the Lord knows when that life should end. In the death of a son the father suffers more than the son. **Thou shalt not kill.**

Adultery is the only sex sin spoken of in the Ten Commandments. Does this mean that adultery is the worst sex sin or does this mean that adultery is the mother of many sins? I tend to believe, the latter. Adultery has the potential to corrupt the plan of salvation. Adultery defies the principle of trust that is vital for progress in the church family, as well as in the home. The family is an institution created by God. Our spiritual and physical attitude regarding the family reflects our spiritual attitude about our trust we place in God.

We must ask ourselves, "Can we trust a godly-structured family?" God says that a family should be composed of a male and female. God says that a child should leave his or her biological family so that this union may be complete. God also provides this family with a spiritual structure that displays our trust in Him. This spiritual display should serve as a tool by which our young children may come to believe in God. Our attitudes about our godly role display our attitude towards the wisdom of God. Do we truly believe that we serve an all-wise God?

Beware if this is a question in your mind. It is a chance that it is a question in the mind of your youth also. Then we must ask ourselves can we not trust a godly structured family. Could it be that adultery tells our young and others that God's rules and social rules do not matter? Does adultery teach our young to be cold blooded and deceitful. Does accepting our God given rules teach our young that it's ok to choose an ungodly role for life? **Thou shalt not commit adultery.**

Stealing is the act, of taking something that belongs to someone else without the permission of the owner or responsible person.

Some people may feel that stealing is not a bad sin, as long as you get away with it. *Stealing represents the presence of the most ungodly person on the face of the earth*. He is ungodly because God is love. A thief has no love for his fellow man or his God. He is a major factor in the demise of the ministries of God. He is a thorn found in the side of God's children. His victims are those who struggle to live according to God's will. This makes him a double hardship for God. When you steal from God's people you hinder the salvation of the world.

When you steal in church, you support the kingdom of Satan. This includes things that belong to your brother, your sister your church and last but not least, your God. When our young children see us joyfully supporting thieves in church (the number one place where it should not be allowed) it tends to justify them supporting gangs that support stealing outside the church. No Godly institution should be an example for stealing. To be a fraud or to embezzle, is to steal. It is to treat a fellow man unfair. This is what God do not support. **Thou shalt not steal.**

When I consider the many scriptures in the Bible that expresses God's feeling of a liar when one of Christ's apostles sought safety by telling a lie, I am amazed by the wording of the ninth commandment.

As a Sunday school teacher, of adolescents, I was told by a deacon, who was ten years my senior and who was also the superintendent of the Sunday school, "Don't be telling those young people not to lie." When I asked him why, his answer was, "There will come a time when they will need to lie."

Scripture teaches Christians how to live their lives so that lies are not needed. The ninth commandment is exactly what God wants and needs His people to understand. He did not make man to place hardships on fellow man. A false anything is contrary to the truth or fact. This makes a false witness, a liar and more. A false witness is treacherous. His life represents and his voice advocates faith in an opposing spirit of God. And, he is a killer of both spirit and body of man. Jesus Christ, the son of God fell victim to false witness unto death. Christian jury members of ten allow themselves to fall victim to false witness unto the death of another. To error is false witness and are often declared as being a lie. We error when we speak out of ignorance. The scripture, II Peter 1:1-5 reminds us that knowledge is a means by which our faith may be enhanced.

Often the devil strives to keep God's people defenseless by keeping them ignorant. In the church this behavior is accomplished by not providing reports of finances and other information where errors may be amplified. Thus, those seeking the knowledge appear to be liars, as well as trouble makers. **Thou shalt not bear false witness against thy neighbor.**

The tenth commandment may be conceived as the reminder command. With it man may cure himself of the sin virus. If taken religiously, it will prevent sexual desires that could lead to adultery. The "crave" that prevents theft, the envy that leads to death. When we keep the tenth commandment, we honor our father in heaven and on earth when we take heed to advice given by them. **Thou shalt not covet thy neighbor's house; thou shalt not covet thy neighbor's wife, or his manservant, or his maid servant, or his ox, or his ass, or anything that is thy neighbors.**

Summary

An appropriate summary for the last five commandments: The Golden Rule may be found in the gospel of St. Matthew 8: 12. Therefore, all things whatsoever ye would, that man should do to you, do you even so to them; for this is the law and the prophet.

Spiritual and physical death

Webster defines kill as to put to death or to deprive of life. This is very simple definition to understand—or is it? Murder, on the other hand, is defined as the unlawful killing of one person by another. Trying to distinguish between to kill and to murder can become as difficult as trying to identify the front side of a basketball. As Christians, we do not think of man as being one man but two men. Often the question comes up asking, "Is to kill and to murder the same?" Murder is defined as the crime of unlawfully killing a person. Murder appears to be more of a sociological term that can be justified by a judicial process. God said thou shalt not kill. This should be the position of all Church assemblies. Killing and murder hinder the maturity of the physical, as well as, the spiritual man. No man knows the full consequences of violating God's laws.

The distastefulness of killing or murdering is that it has the many negative attitudes which are associated with the behavior. Envy, jealousy, arrogance, selfishness, fearfulness, insanity, rage, anger, etc. The list may go on and on. It lacks the compassion of the consideration that God has shown time and time again for His people.

Many Soldiers would like to know if they are wrong for killing as a soldier in the United States Army. The answer to that question is yes, because killing is contrary to God's will. However, they will not be held accountable for the sins of their country.

Jesus did not come to destroy spiritual or social laws. Christians are responsible for supporting social efforts to eliminate evil in the world. As Christians we are to give unto our government and to God what is due. It is the responsibility of Christian citizens to put Christian people in office, the same as it is for our Church assembles. When we do not do so, the government will pay. Sin does not go unpunished. Your reward and punishment will be based on your support of good and evil men that serve our country.

There is no godly support for man or country (by way of

the government) to kill. However, there is godly support of a universal effort to enhance righteousness. The Lord, who was wise enough to give life, is the only one wise enough to take life. Our heavenly Father is a loving father who knows all and sees all. He is a father that will give every opportunity for each and every one of his sons and daughters to enter into His kingdom in heaven. It is the spiritual man that God waits patiently to repent. Only God and God alone knows when there is no hope for repentance for man and the world. No man nor country knows the point when man or this world has reached the point of no repentance.

Who has the authority or the audacity to rob God of one of his children to return home? He will not find him blameless. When Christians do not support truth, justice and righteousness in our schools, in our courts, in our social events, we are less valuable to God and His kingdom than the common atheist. All death administrated by man has a negative effect on the ministries of God, country, and fellow man.

Church and home adultery

Adultery is willful sexual intercourse with someone other than one's wife or husband. Jesus expanded the act to include lusting. (Matthew 5:28) The Mosaic Law put both parties to death when caught in the act of adultery. Even though adultery may be the mother of all sex sins, Christ declared that man could not justify killing those who were caught in such acts. All sex sins defy family order as God propose, regardless of it being the Christian family, which is the nucleus of the church family, which is the nucleus of a Christian society.

The basic concept of the family, as the basic social unit, may be traced back to the creation. Genesis 2:24 A man shall leave his mother and his father and cleave unto his wife and they shall be as one. The "as one" eliminates the superiority or the inferiority of either. Genesis 1: 22 God brought a woman unto the man. God gave man his choice of trees to eat from. God gave man his choice of gender to build a family. There are things about the male gender that woman can only speculate about. There are things about the female gender that man can only speculate about. This choice, by God, that a family should have two genders and two difference of knowledge of the two genders, is a vital source of knowledge for family life, as well as child training. Sex is spoken of in terms of conception and that the woman's desires should be to her husband. The order to multiply is one of the many responsibilities God placed on the family.

Adultery is a sin. As all other sins adultery is capable of planting seeds by which other sins may germinate. This sin is just as destructive in the church family as it is in the social family. There are severe destructive side effects to the ministries of the church when this sin is ignored by the congregation. Adultery is to the family what a thief is to the church. Adultery robs a family of all the sacred resources that are vital for unity and growth. Adultery displays that breaking rules are acceptable. This can prove to be a destructive tool for family, church and the nation. Self-gratification is placed above the unit as well as above God.

This is an unnecessary source of division in the congregation when a church leader has a reputation for this sin. Your leaders should be of good report.

This is the sin that makes other sex offenders justify their sins. Report of adultery, child molestation, homosexuality and incest should not be condoned. Your leaders represent you as a Church. It is your responsibility as a church member to proclaim to the world that these behaviors do not have the approval of God or the Church of Christ. As a Christian you should hold the church's reputation at a higher standard (or in higher esteem) than your own.

Adultery often declares a lie as being an accepted course of action. It displays to youth what is and what should be as a myth. It declares that loyalty has only an imaginary existence. It puts family members at odds with each other at home and in the church. Adultery destroys communication. It creates an environment that is not productive for learning. It forces family members to make serious choices that otherwise would not be necessary.

As Christians we approve God when we approve truth and righteousness. When we disapprove truth and righteousness, we disapprove God. When we approve those of bad report we place the church, our children, as well as our brothers and sisters, in harm's way. Remember, these persons you approve for your positions in your assemblies will be instructing your children, who feel that you have approved their behavior.

Church and social stealing

Thou shalt not steal is simple. Thou shall not take anything that belongs to another person without the prior approval of that person or organization. Stealing is the most destructive sin to the ministries of God. All five of the brotherhood sins, which are the last five commandments, have a crippling effect for God's earthly kingdom becoming as His kingdom in heaven. What's wrong with stealing? Let's count the ways.

A thief is a cold blooded person. He has no compassion for God or fellow man. He is all that God is not. A thief has a selfish nature. He takes pride in his ability, as well as his associate's ability, to take from God and man. He has no concern or compassion for the struggles and hardships that man has endured to obtain their possessions or their wealth. God's plan of salvation or man's plan of survival is conceived as a source by which a thief may satisfy their selfishness.

A thief puts his quest to obtain before God. Those who obtain contrary to the will of God are not successful. Successful persons are those who are able to obtain within the legal bounds of man and God. Many thieves appear as being successful. They often boast of their success as a means of obtaining other positions. This occurs in the case of the secular positions as well as non-secular positions. Those who obtain positions or possessions contrary to the will of God will not only bring those practices with him but, will also teach them to others.

Those who place the love of money above the love of God have no love for the ministries of God. He has no love for the people of God. Church unity and church peace is often a thing of the past. If the church is viewed as "a child of God" any person who is willing to divide the child has no love for the child. Any person who does not have the wisdom to administrate without division should be wise enough to remove himself. The badge of courage of thieves, which is of Satan, must be met and challenged with the good courage of God. This is the act of a mature Christian. Never under estimate the destructiveness, and the determination of a thief in church; for he is as all thieves, will place his life, the life of the church, your life and the welfare of your loved ones, in danger to accomplish his objectives. As a Christian you should be just as determined as the thief when it comes to accomplishing the objectives of God.

Those who are of bad report must be removed from office. However, the church does not have the authority to remove even the thief from the assemblies of God. It is the responsibility of the church to bring in members and not to become a stumbling block for unbelievers. Those of bad report will always be of bad report. Remember the scriptures look among you and selects those of good report to place in leadership positions. For some persons it takes over forty years to repent. God alone should have the power over death for He alone knows when repentance is impossible.

Who will open and close the church? Trust me to determine who speaks or doesn't speak to the congregation. Trust me to determine when the congregation should have meetings. Trust me to declare who are the real "devils" in the congregation. Trust me, for I know what's best for you and the church. This is the greatest indication of an ungodly person. Sinful persons request of you things that are contrary to the scriptures.

Psalm 118: 8

It is better to take refuge in the Lord than to trust in man. Jeremiah 17:5 Cursed is the man who puts his trust in man and makes flesh his strength, whose heart turns away from the Lord. Roman 8:18 tells us that we are not led by man, but by the spirit of God.

Church thieves request things of you that only God should request. (Thou shalt not have no other God before God. Such a request is offensive to God and Christians.) James 3:2 In many things we offend all, if any man offend not in words the same is a perfect man.

Witnessing and Lying

Scripture teaches us, "thou shalt not lie." The ninth commandment takes us far beyond the lie. God displays an innate ability to deal with a store house of ill behavior in one statement. A lie is a false creation of the mind. It is an "unplayed" scene or role or a spoken or heard statement, stated as the truth. Jesus said, "I am the truth and the light." The unbeliever, often speaks of not believing in the unseen yet, he is willing to put his trust in the unseen lie. When we trust in the truth we trust in God. When we trust in God, we trust in His plan of salvation.

God's plan of salvation drains the lie of its value. Those who go contrary to the will of God often seek security in lies. As Christians, we teach the plan of salvation so that the lie has no value for us. Lying is false witness. When we lie, we bear witness to the presence of something that is not true. The life span of a lie or the destructive nature of a lie is controlled by the lie itself and not the liar. All lies are against God. Lies display a lack of trust in God. We as Christian must bear witness to the presence of God in our lives. We bear witness when we display that living our life as God would have us is not only possible but it is also rewarding.

When we bear false witness against our neighbor, we do a disservice to the plan of salvation. We display a lack of trust in God. The ninth commandment makes us mindful that God is concerned for us and He is also concerned about us being supportive of the truth. Jesus, in his day, was a victim of false witness. False witness harms the children of God. As Christians we are expected to speak what we know and refrain from what we think and to pray for the inspiration of the Holy Spirit to show us the difference.

Witnesses are often tempted to rely on what we think to be the truth rather than what we know to be the truth. This is a false witness. God does not expect for us to believe what we have not seen in man. He expects that we should be mindful of the fact that there are things beyond our knowledge and He expects us not to move in the realm of speculation. This is the only time when the phrase, "let loose and let God," should be applied. God expects His people to work to enhance the kingdom of God. He expects prayer for the courage to stand against those who will give earthly gifts that are contrary to the will of God. As a disciple we must pray for courage that exceeds the courage of those who practice works for Satan.

The mindset of covetousness

Covet or covetousness, is a strong desire to possess something that belongs to another. This desire is present in the behavior of thieves, adulterers, killers and false witnesses. In every instance those are the same seeds of these sins. It is a metaphysical process that involves an analytical evaluation of the worth of God, man and self. Covetousness is spiritually self-destructive.

In phase one of this process man reevaluates his belief in God. He may ask himself these questions. Is there a God and do I believe in Him? Is His wisdom capable of providing the quality of life that I am seeking? Is He a watchful God? Is He judgmental? Will I truly be punished and what will be the severity of my punishment? Am I willing to accept condemnation and am I ready to risk my salvation?

The second phase begins with the conclusion that the worth of God, man or beast will be placed secondary to this endeavor. At this point in the church, the resource for the ministries becomes the focal point. These persons have no power of their own. They seek among you and find those of little faith to perform the acts of the devil. Often this involves destroying the reputation of the good, minimizing the value of the ministries of God and encouraging the weak to go contrary to the Ten Commandments in many endeavors.

It is just as important to know the nature of a godly person as it is to know the nature of the ungodly. The godly person is meek. There is a difference between meek and weak. A weak person is easily broken. A meek person is domesticated because he believes in following the rules. He is tame because he allows God's rules to charter his steps. Often evil persons will present them as subdued and ignorant because he will not break the laws of those governing. A godly person will not save himself at the cost of division. The evil person knows this and often uses this against the church. The meek relies on the fact that the majority of any church congregation should believe in what is right. This is how a weak Christian, a no vote Christian, "Let loose and let God Christian," allows evil to control God's churches. A godly person often reads scriptures that support the Ten Commandments.

SECTION 2

The Christian Family

Webster defines the family as parents and their children. This may be a definition that a Christian may be able to apply in their union. However, there must be a clear understanding about the term "parents." For all Christian purpose, parents are a mother and a father. Because of the growing diversity of family life in our society today, even the simplest of terms must be explained. The Christian family must consist of a male father and a female mother. This concept comes from Genesis 2:24, Even though the term wife has been distorted by ungodly unions, this is the combination of a family that God commanded.

Corinthians 6:14 brings attention to very important elements of a Christian family. A Christian family should be evenly yoked. This means that the mother and the father should believe that the principles of God will be the ultimate respected course of action for family behavior. These principles should be seen in lifestyle and taught to the children. These principles should be so lived that they become the norm for the family.

There are social roles each member of the family must accept as the will of God once married. The husband and the wife become as one. I Corinthians 7:4 The wife has no power of her own body, but the husband and likewise also the husband hath not power of his own body, but the wife. The scripture tells the wife to submit yourself to your husband and the husband is head of the wife. The scripture requires the husband to love his wife as their own body. Ephesians 5:21-28. The scripture demands that neither husband nor wife is not to commit adultery. These commands are set in place for the welfare of the family as a whole.

When the husband or wife abuses Christian family principles, children question the value of family and social rules. When the wife abuses principles of the family concerning the husband, she places in question, the value of male gender by the male child. When the husband abuses principles of the family concerning the wife, he places in question, the value of the female gender by the female child.

Adultery is the most destructive behavior that happens to a family. The destructiveness of adultery has the tendency to filter into destructive social behavior. Every sin lived by a sinner is taught by that sinner to another. Adultery teaches one to lie, to steal, to disrespect rules, as well as, undermine loyalty inside and outside the family.

A non-Christian family is apart from God. A Christian family is a sacred family. It has the will of God as its director. It is the "golden cell" of a healthy society.

The spiritual composition of the Christian family is composed where the wiles of Satan may not pierce the walls of its domain. There is a productive reason for every request of God. These requests are both productive for maintaining family and social stability.

Man shall leave his mother and father and select a wife and they shall become one. A family should and must be bound by the ties of love. Sex is a by-product of this union. And, with this by-product, the family is capable of multiplying when this Christian family has been faithful in their composition of the family. Their tact of learning and training becomes a family experience.

Each spouse has the opportunity to learn about the difference in gender as well as teach that difference to their young. By the female exercising her Christian right of silence in church, she protects her family from division from the devil. Because of the love the husband has for the wife, her wishes are fulfilled in the home as well as in the church. Our faithfulness to God gives us the wisdom to appreciate those things He asks of us.

CHAPTER 4

To the Church

To the Congregations of God that confesses to be members of God's Holy Church, be not deceived. You are a special society, set aside by God, to fulfill the purpose by which Christ was born. The Church is God's continual effort to save you and the world from condemnation.

In the Garden of Eden the serpent voiced his opinion about God's right, to be the God of man. When man obtained the knowledge of good and evil he also obtained the capability to select who he wished to serve. God would like to honor that wish. Now God is offering Himself to be your protector, your way maker, your God, if you are willing to be his preached nation. This means that you must first be willing to accept Him as the ultimate authority in your life and secondly you must be willing to support His efforts to save mankind and the world from eternal condemnation. When we accept Jesus Christ as our Lord and Savior, we also accept God as our Lord and Savior. God so loved the world that He gave his son so that we may know what He would have us to do as his preached nation.

The son of God was sent to save lost souls and to honor His father which art in heaven by living, teaching, and dying so that the world would know the will of His father in heaven. Before the death of Jesus, he established a unique group of people, a sacred people, and a people who are able to accept the way he lived, the things that he taught as being the true message from God. In the words of the son of man, he declared that these sacred people will be called the Church. The Church is composed of sacred people who were called out by the sacred son, to complete a sacred work. Congregations are a special people who do not hear the words of those who speak contrary to the will of God. You and your efforts should be as sacred as the procedure in the Garden of Eden. Only godly people do godly work.

Chief leadership positions in the church or "Garden of Eden" positions cannot allow the ungodly to preside. Making decisions about these positions should be as if the life of the church mission depends on them because the success of a godly mission depends on godly leadership.

Churches should make sure that leaders are full of the Holy Ghost. And, in cases of poor decision making, church members should not feel out of place by requesting their removal. Most ungodly persons are masters of disguise. God trusted Adam one time. After which, he removed him from the Garden of Eden and the sacredness of the garden. As members of God's Church you cannot take the chance of leaving those who act contrary to God's will to remain in the church's sacred places. Leadership positions in church are also God's Garden of Eden positions.

Allow the scripture to determine who serve you. Always leave the scripture-qualified person in that position. He will be capable of working with a more intelligent person. If a more intelligent person is not willing to work with him for the church, he will not work for the advancement of the church in that position without him. The devil would have you to believe that no one lives up to scripture standard. There are persons in each congregation that are qualified according to the scripture. Seek among you and find them. The next lie they will tell is that those persons are not intelligent enough to perform.

Congregations, "The success of your ministries will be no more successful as your determination to place godly people in your sacred positions." This is the beginning place for church success. Congregations, "You are important to God." When you vote for a godly person you vote for God. You must be of good courage. If a member approaches you about someone stealing or committing adultery, that person is not necessarily the devil.

The person that sins is the one who caused the chaos to come about.

Faith

When we speak of faith in God, we are referring to a belief in God or our confident attitude towards God. This involves our commitment to His will for our life. Hebrew 11: 1 defines faith as being the substance of things hoped for, the evidence of things not seen. This is the foundation by which Christians place their hope in God. This hope becomes a physical substance from things unseen. This is the thing that divides the good from the bad. This is the substance that makes man live a righteous life. This is also a thing that the atheist and some scientists cannot justify. They are not able to take the physical and natural attributes of the unseen and dedicate their body and soul to that principle. With faith we strive for righteousness, in our struggles we justify our faith.

Enoch, which was the son of Jared and the father of Methuselah, lived a righteous life. His goal was to please God at any cost. Enoch was "translated" or was taken directly into the presence of God. He did not experience death. His life represents the substance of things unseen. In the Ten Commandments God stated his position--His desires for His people and His world.

As time passed God's words were altered to the will and ways of man so that man may decode what man had encoded in His word. The presence of the son of God was merited for the salvation of the world. As believers in His word, Hebrews 12:2 tells us that we must fix our eyes on Jesus, the author and perfector of our faith. This represents God's physical attempt to satisfy the materialistic mind of His presence.

Faith in God separates the world into two distinct worlds. One world who believes in God's plan for the salvation of man and the preservation of the world. The other world advocates a somewhat "survivor of the fit" plan. This world we know, and expect, to be contrary to God's will. However, what we do not expect is different levels of faith and non-believers in the congregations of God. Non-believers often select Christian congregations to prey on. In many of these congregations there are levels of faith within the congregation that all churches must be able to deal with respectfully. Faith levels cannot be seen. However, the behavior of these levels may be seen.

Faith, Level One

Thy shall worship, God and God alone

Characteristic wise, this level believes in the leader and supports the leader one hundred percent. Many of the followers lack a true knowledge or concern about what the church is about. They like to be seen or known as one of the leader's favorite. They defy anyone who defies the leader. The leader is a sacred rat, who has all power and authority over the church assembly. To them everything he does is condoned by God. He may lie, steal, commit adultery, covet, bribe, kill, and misuse his sisters and brothers in Christ for the so-called well-being of the church. They never act contrary to the will of this leader. When the leader is ungodly there will always be dissension between this faith level and the third faith level.

This level tends to worship the leader. If the leader is godly, they worship God. If the leader is ungodly they worship the devil. The scripture tells us that when we worship man we worship that man's God. Under good Christian leadership this faith level is a productive force for Christ. When leadership is bad they are without a doubt the most destructive force in the church. This is the group that the godly and ungodly leaders target first. This level supports the growth of good or evil in the church.

If an ungodly leader remains in office for a substantial amount of time, the church runs the risk of becoming completely ungodly. Ungodly leaders discourage the presence or support of the godly in the church program. At this point ignorance and fear becomes the criteria for growth in this faith level. Growth of this faith level becomes the criteria of an ungodly leader's existence. The sheep of Christ become his sheep and the church resources become his resources.

"Let loose and let God become their battle cry."

The ungodly usually uses this statement to encourage Christians not to get involved actively in resolving issues. The "Great Commission" is not an inactive mission.

John 10:16 tells us that Christ laid His life down for His sheep. Here Christ proclaims ownership and love for sheep of two different fold. One fold that has not yet heard his voice--a confused fold. Yet, Christ made it clear to Peter that out of the love that He has for him, he expects him to feed His sheep. Christ was not asking Peter. He was telling Peter to preach the gospel pure and simple.

Many local churches have failed when it comes to feeding God's sheep. Those of little faith have similar attributes of sheep. Those of little faith will be submissive to whoever is carrying the staff or whoever has been put in leadership roles by the congregation. They feel that when man obtains a godly position in the church assembly, it is ungodly not to support them. They feel that these persons are exempt from following the will of God as written in the scriptures. They place their lives in the hands of someone who they feel are closer in touch with God, and the money, than they are.

Like a child, people at this level do not hold these leadership persons accountable for their actions and they feel that anyone who does so is evil. They trust whole-heartedly in their words and actions even when they are contrary with the will of God. They trust them when they tell them that God has made them head of his church. They trust them when they tell them that God has given them the power of authority in the church. They trust them when they tell them that they have a closer relationship with God than they do. They make it clear to them that they do not have the kind of relationship with God to be able to understand basic scripture. They have not learned the difference in turning their life over to man and turning their life over to God. They like the praise of man more than the praise of God.

They do not understand that there is no difference in a church leader and the corner gang leader when the church leader goes contrary to the will of God. When the children of church members are not able to see the difference in church leaders and gang leaders, they choose to follow the corner gang leader who offers them temporary solutions to their problems. These are the first members ungodly leaders solicit for support. These are the sheep of God that need a greater passion from the soldiers and saints of God. It is vital that every ordinance, covenant, prayer or rule in God's assembly are designed to protect those who have not yet the understanding and wisdom to support God's program. At this level, ungodly leaders serve as a stumbling block for those who need to be fed. And, those who need to be fed serve as a stumbling block for ungodly leaders. Ultimately, the congregation as a whole, is responsible for not removing ungodly leaders from leadership roles.

When rules of the congregation are designed to protect

those of little faith, the church moves forward at a greater pace. The devil obtains power in the church when members of little faith are not protected.

What part of this level displays faith in God? This level believes in working to obtain what they have even though they will support their leaders whom they know are stealing. Those who work do not take from their fellow man. This is Godly.

Biblically, St. Peter nor any of the apostles, cannot be identified with this level of faith. This level of faith characterizes the actions of the apostle Judith or the Israelites, who remain in the wilderness for forty years, members may remain at this level for forty years or more.

Faith Level 2

Be not wise in your own eyes

There are many phrases and attributes that can be tied to this faith level. Faith level three will refer to them as whispering Smith. Historically, they may be classified as a sunshine soldier. Biblically, they may be referred to as a lukewarm Christian. They believe in God. They know the scripture. In a pleasant environment they will teach the gospel pure and simple. They even secretly have praise for those who stand up for Christ. They are a blessing to a congregation, under good Christian leadership.

However, under ungodly leadership, those people are useless. They not only know Christ, they also know the devil. They fear the devil more so than they fear God. They shy away from meetings to avoid taking an open stand. They are not to be found at voting time. This is the group that is basically responsible for ungodly leaders getting in office and staying in office. Ungodly leaders declare that this group is of their fold. The ultimate objective of the ungodly is to obtain votes to continue functioning as they have. They will accept bribes, rather than anger God's adversaries. Basically, this class has decided that the best way to protect themselves is to remain silent. The additional hardship they place on their sisters and brothers in Christ are tolerated. In the secular world they are "in the know," yet, they will not share what they know with sisters and brothers so they may also avoid the wilds of the devil. This group is so firmly set in their ways that neither group will campaign for their support.

These are they that believe in God. They have moved to the level in their faith where they know the difference in worshiping God and worshiping man. They would get involved in kingdom building upon request. They strive to live their lives to the glory of God. Their effectiveness in enhancing the kingdom of God begins and ends with their safety. They are usually highly skilled individuals and are truly capable of moving the church forward. They will stand up for Christ on popular issues, but they will allow the devil to be victorious on unpopular issues.

These are they, who are knowledgeable of many issues that will negatively affect their fellow man, but often they choose to watch their devastation, rather than given them a helping hand. They also know the consequences are going contrary to the will of the ungodly and in a battle for the Lord, they are useless. They will run and hide and deny God His victory. They believe in and know the teachings of God. They are even capable of preserving the saintly nature of the body of Christ. They will even secretly praise the soldiers of the cross for their bravery.

Faith Level 3

Love One Another

Major attributes of those on this level love Christ, believe in what He said, has the courage to stand, and are willing to endure hardship for the sake of the church assembly. These are the long lived experienced Christian. They are honest and sincere about what they believe. They have unity among themselves. They do not put their trust in man and have a sincere remorse for those who do put their trust in man. They are very observant of God's commandments. They despise those who misuse God's resources. They lack compassion for sinners. They are the number one adversary of ungodly leaders.

These are they that strive to live their lives for the glory of God. They are the soldiers of God. They have those inside and outside of the faith of God to contend with. Those who are of blind faith hate their very presence. They are not satisfied with just being mesmerized by the word. They would rather see the word of God as being a part of the body of Christ. They seek ways to enhance the kingdom of God and at the same time enhance the quality of life on earth. They are the people who believe tithes and offerings should be used to enhance the kingdom of God. The Church never has too much as long as there are social, judicial and economical injustices, there are no extra resources. They believe in seeking out and destroying obstacles that hinder the growth of the church body. They believe in accountability as well as respectful leaders, including themselves. They believe in an open book policy and that secrets are the source of many internal conflicts in the body of Christ.

They believe in equality, setting rules and following rules by all. They believe that males should not be in a position to provide favors for females. They believe that the Ten Commandments, with the first commandment and the second commandment, should be seen as rules governing the lives of Church leaders. They cannot be bribed.

Last, but not least, they understand what it means to lift Christ. They understand that voting for what is right inside and outside of the church is the major work of lifting up Christ. However, preaching and teaching the gospel purely is a close second. They believe those who are not strong enough to stand for what is right in the midst of obstacles need additional training in the word of God. They are more likely to respond boldly to events of importance.

This level of faith may be viewed as an example with Peter's faith walk during the time when he cut the soldier's ear off.

Faith Level 4

Webster's dictionary defines saint as a person of great purity, who has been recognized as such; a person who has died and is in heaven. My definition of a saint is a person of great purity, dead or alive. Saints obtain attributes of God during their life on earth. God is spirit. The spirit of God in saints make them who they are. This implies that there are no saints on earth.

There are saints that dwell among us. There are also

demons that dwell among us. Often our selfishness, our quest for self-worth, our lack of faith in good spirits blinds us of their presence. What makes their presence even more difficult to perceive is that demons evil spirits disguise themselves as good spirits.

These is the person who walks softly, speak the true and love the Lord. They inwardly rejoice at the mere sight of those that are rewarded for their Christian walk. They have the words and wisdom of God to move things forward. They are compassionate but saddened when Satan can receive a majority vote, especially in a religious environment. Like God, they expect more from those that proclaim the gospel. Often, that is too much to ask.

They are discouraged by leaders that do not follow through on projects and make promises that they have no intension of keeping. His heart is saddened at those that have the audacity to misuse God and God's resources. Their dreams are not for them, but for the world. Their resources are often depleted resolving the problem of others.

These are they that bear extreme hardships. They have the power and blessings of God. Their success is despised by evil doers. Often obstacles are placed in their way to discredit the principals by which they live. These people's lives are hated by those who practice the works of Satan. These persons are the number two target of ungodly leaders to be removed from a Christian environment. They are the first that would say, "Come unto Christ all of you that is burdened and heavy labored and God will give you rest." These are the saints of God's kingdom.

Peter represents this level when he stood before the congregation on the day of Pentecost.

CHAPTER 5

Ships of Zion

The voice of today's Church are becoming increasingly silent in a world that is becoming increasingly sinful. The principles of the world of darkness are successfully placing dark shadows upon the principles of the world of light.

The Church was designed by Christ to shine as a light so man may see his way to the holy city of God. It is written that the open gates of hell shall not prevail. Now is the time that each member shall pull up anchors and be about the business of the Church. Each member of the Church of Christ has been molded by God into an individual vessel capable of transporting themselves and others from life to eternal life.

In this sense these vessels will be referred to as "ships." Man is referred to as a vessel by the scriptures. Ships transport people. Every church congregation should develop skills to equip every vessel with the knowledge of God.

The four ships of Zion: worship (God ship), fellowship,

discipleship and stewardship. Each of these Christian "ships" have the capability of embarking souls to the place of eternal life. These ships are of the same spirit.

When the word of God is used for kindling, the power of the word directs their way.

Wor-ship

Webster's definition of worship is reverence for a sacred object: high esteem or devotion for a person; to revere; attend a religious service. This is a good secular definition of worship. However, this definition leaves too many ways that a person can miss boarding the "Worship" ship of Zion. God is not an object, God is a spirit. The spirit of God determines the degree of sacredness of any person, place or thing. To board the ship of Zion you must not worship sacred objects. We worship the god that provides the sacredness of these objects.

God is not an object. God is a spirit. The spirit of God determines the degree of sacredness of any person, place or thing. To board the Ship of Zion you must not worship sacred objects. We worship the God that provides the sacredness of these objects.

Worshipping God for many of us have become precious moments. These moments have become so precious to us that we have acquired a selfish nature about them. When we should worship God has become a needless issue of division.

Who is truly a member of the church of Christ? Who is more capable of directing our faith? The question that comes to my mind is, "How can you divide one father, one son, one spirit who is on one accord?"

Where should we worship God? The obvious answers to the question would be in those places which has been set aside for and in His holy name. Nothing is holy apart from God. We worship in places where we have covenant with God that we will advocate and praise the excellence of His ways. This includes in our hearts, souls spirits and minds as well as in places of our secular choices.

How do we worship God?

We worship God in spirit and in truth. We worship God in the spirit of all of His natural unbelievable, believable attributes. Then we worship Him in the spirit of all of His loving unbelievable, believable moral attributes. We worship Him because He is God, the almighty! And, he is that all by Himself. We worship Him when it is taxing. We worship Him when it is not taxing. Taxing ways of worshipping God would be when we have the opportunity to advance His ways, by being of good courage and choosing truth and righteousness in our places of worship, schools, work places and communities. We worship God when it is not taxing when we sing praises to His name and when we are in His presence and in the presence of other believers.

When do we worship God?

We worship God in the morning. We worship God in the evening. We worship God in the night. We worship God all the days of our lives.

Christian Steward-ship

A good secular definition of stewardship is a manager of another person's financial affairs. From many pulpits I have heard, "Giving God ten percent of your earnings makes you a good Christian steward." A non-secular definition of stewardship or a Christian definition of stewardship may be defined as the management of God's work throughout the Church. What this means is that paying tithes is the mere beginning of a Christian responsibility of being a good Christian steward. God has left His works to be completed by the Church. You are a member of the church. This means God has appointed all Christians, collectively, as well as individually, to be His stewards on earth. Stewardship is not an option. This is mandatory.

Managing God's works and managing God's resources is all inclusive. This means you cannot effectively manage God's works without managing God's resources. Managing God's works involves a place to worship, a place to train, and a place to serve.

As a good steward, it is your responsibility to promote the wisdom of putting God-fearing people in leadership positions, and to promote the courage to remove them when they are found of bad report.

The most cherished attribute of God is His sheep. Being a good steward involves not allowing wolves to scatter His sheep. Supporting anyone who scatters God's sheep is contrary to being a good steward. The foundation of the church is not based on leadership. It is based on discipleship.

God has one Church. Christ established one Church. God the father, God the son, God the Holy Spirit, is also one.

All local church assemblies belong to this one Church. The greater work that God has for the Church is outside local Church assembly. The biggest lie that the Satan's forces have sold the Christian force is that we are separate, but equal. "Divide and conquer" is among the oldest military strategy on record. Division represents the presence of evil. A demon is one who speaks contrary to the will of God.

Christ's work inside Church assemblies involves unifying the Church assembly. Unifying Church assembly involves unifying faith levels. Unifying faith levels involves preaching the gospel pure and simple. Preaching the gospel involves selecting leaders that are full of the Holy Ghost. A good steward recognizes that the faith level of Christians vary. It is the work of a good steward to gives tithes of love as needed for Christian growth. Christian growth is vital for Christian unity. The forces of evil cannot pierce the shield of Christian unity. A good steward is mindful of the dividing forces of evil. The devil may wear the veil of truth and righteousness but, that veil must be removed to perform the deeds of Satan. The deeds of Satan is always contrary to the will of God. The devil has no power of his own. He needs the power Christ has given to you to enhance the kingdom of God in order to accomplish his evil ends.

The support of righteousness is a good stewardship. As a Christian steward it is your responsibility to protect God's resources. When Christ gives you resources He expects for you to increase those resources and use them to perform His works. Your responsibility as a Christian steward is to demand accountability more so than you would with your own funds, for Christ's work is far more important than yours!

The work of a Christian steward outside church assembly increases God's kingdom. It may be referred to as the greater work Christ gave reference. Often, as Christians, we turn our attention to secular systems for food, clothing, shelter, jobs, educational programs, finances, and social needs, legal and protective support. Even as Christians, we grumble about the inability of these secular systems to perform these tasks effectively. It is the responsibility of Christian stewards to serve in secular positions to perform the works of Christ.

The non-secular Christian population, which is twice the population of the voting population of the United States, is more than capable of performing these tasks in the name of our Lord and Savior, Jesus Christ. If and when we as an assembly in Christ, join forces to rid God's sanctuaries of ungodly leadership, we will be capable of doing all these things and more. As Christian stewards we must put on the full armor of the spirit and be about the business of Christ.

The most common places and events where Christians openly support the devil instead of lifting up Christ is in Christian council meetings. For Christ this must be a disheartening affair.

Not having the courage to do what's right is a common behavior of a first and second faith level Christian. First faith level members lift Satan up out of ignorance and a strong desire to please leadership. A second faith level member will vote for wrong out of a fear of ungodly leadership. This is the faith level that would refuse to vote either way or they will run and hide. The third faith level is going to lift Christ up even if it kills them or somebody else. And, they have a strong dislike for those who don't.

As a good steward, you must learn to identify the faith level of your brothers and sisters in Christ. As a good steward, this is vital for you. It is your responsibility to place these persons in positions where they may serve, grow in faith, and be a positive force in the church mission. Identifying the faith level of your brothers and sisters is a vital attribute for you to perform the most important service to God and that is to remove ungodly leaders from positions that demand a person of good report.

Understanding Christian stewardship for a church or a disciple, perhaps is the most rewarding possession that a church or a disciple may have for the enhancement of the Kingdom of God. In learning how to be a good steward, we learn how to protect ourselves as well as God Church from the ways of the devil. Webster's dictionary define, steward as being a manager of another's financial affairs; a person responsible for maintaining household affairs. Christian leaders, in many cases declare that managing church affairs should be left to assign persons. This should be the first sign that your leader is not a Christian leader. Chaotic condition in our lives as well as in our Church is because we are poor stewards.

As far as a Christians are concerned, stewardship involves accepting the responsibility of managing God's resources of the Church. Stewardship is not an option, it is a responsibility that could endanger your salvation. Being a steward is part of believing the gospel. Be not deceive, every member of the Church is a steward. Paying your tithes is a small part of you being a good steward.

The two greatest part of Christian stewardship are: 1. that the work of the Church reflect the Character of Christ, and 2. that the resources of God is used to enhance his Kingdom. There are many Scripture of the Old and New Testament revile the will of God,

Regarding stewardship, 1 Corinthians 4: 1 tells' us that

we will be held accountable, for the ministries of Christ, as well as the mysteries of God. Luke 12: 37 tell us as a steward, we will be bless for watching,so we will be aware of the hour of the thief. Matt. 20: 1-16 show that all of God servants are rewarded according to their love for his work, rather than time worked.

Disciple-ship

What is a disciple? A disciple is a person who has by the acceptance of the words and teaching of Jesus Christ, applied for a position in the heavenly Kingdom of God. And, by the power and authority that God has invested in His son, Jesus the Christ, you have by acceptance of His word, become an ambassador of God. Your purpose as an ambassador of God in this foreign land is to equip the lost person with the fortitude capable of them, to return to the land of their heavenly father. You are no longer of this world.

As a disciple of Christ, you have accepted the fact that no principles of endeavor supersedes or are more productive for the enhancement of a kingdom on earth or any kingdom to come. You are not a wimp. You are now a solider of peace, an emancipator, a heart regulator for the down-hearted. Yours is the awesome task of perfecting an imperfect world by encouraging the United Nations to become a member of the "greatest movement on earth," that is the movement for the salvation of the world. You are not a whiner. You cannot be a whiner and an ambassador for God at the same time. You must have the courage to stand for God and for righteousness in the councils all over the world. This is not a *job* for "whimps." This is a job for those who love the almighty God, who love people, who love peace, who love his theory for the salvation of the world. If you do not believe in His principles, you cannot work for Him because you do not believe in Him. These are the makings of disciples for Christ.

A ship is a vessel for deep water transport, or travel. The uniqueness of a ship is as it moves through a journey that is not so smooth, it carries others with it. We must remember that a ship moves best going forward. In times of trouble a ship may sometimes need to go around the problem. But, backing up suddenly is not its best course of action.

Christian disciples are sometimes referred to as a vessel of God. Christian vessels of God have work to do. As a Christian vessel, we work to please God. This work involves studying His word so we may know how to equip ourselves with His wisdom, so that we may live according to His will, so that we may obtain eternal life. We must equip ourselves with His wisdom so that we may be able to teach others the value of living according to His will.

Learning His word, living His word and teaching His word is the work of a disciple.

Discipleship is the process by which a disciple fulfills his commitments, obligations, and responsibilities to God and himself. As a child of God and a member of God's kingdom on earth, all disciples have committed to loving God with all their heart and soul. This love for God commits us to keeping God's commandments, which requires external and internal action. Internally, we must prepare ourselves to accept His will as ours. We must believe in Him as being present, all wise and loving and trust Him. When we come to this point in our lives, we are ready to take actions that will make us more like Him. This is an internal work that provides spiritual growth. It also improves our relationship with God. As a disciple, we work towards improving the quality of our life as we improve the quality of God's kingdom on earth.

External action or commitment may stem from, but is not limited to, being excited by the new found knowledge of how a disciple has improved, his life, is improving his life and can improve the quality of his life. This new found knowledge often sparks a desire of a disciple to share this knowledge and the resource of the knowledge with loved ones, friends and yes, even with enemies.

This is commonly called the plan of salvation.

Christian Fellow-ship

Christian fellowship is a time when those who believe in Christ and the principles He stands for may display his principle in their relationship with others. The common interest of Christian fellowship is Christ. Church socials are one opportunity to fellowship. However, there are many other opportunities in church that may be defined as Christian fellowship events. Church worship services, educational programs and even church business meetings may be viewed as Christian fellowship events.

Christian fellowship is first and foremost a relationship between believers. Therefore, Christian fellowship is a time and opportunity for fellow Christians to rejoice in the qualities of each other that represent the presence of our

Lord and savior in their lives. Christian fellowship at its best enhance relationships not only with each other but also with our heavenly father. Christian fellowship should be a positive learning experience at all times, especially for youth. The motivating factor at these events are Christ and not food.

Hebrews 10; 24-25 Let us consider how to stir up one another to love and good works not neglecting to meet together, as is the habit of some, but encouraging one another.

Congregations that know the value of Christian fellowship provide ongoing activities for their members. As adults and mature Christians, Christian fellowship is an excellent vehicle for bringing young people to Christ. In today's society youth are faced with all kinds of social and relationship issues. A congregation that wishes the best for all the young people will always provide time money and *effort* for activities.

These activities will provide them with the opportunity to associate themselves with friends of parents with similar beliefs. These opportunities are impossible when ungodly people are in leadership. When we take money from a church thief, we take a church thief from our youth. Thieves remove themselves from positions where it is impossible to steal. Those who transgress God's laws live and teach that life they live to others, especially young people.

The scripture tells us to train up a child the way they should go. Christian fellowship is one way we teach Christian youth the value of Christian friends, Christian activities and a Christian environment.

These are the values capable of saving the lives of the young and old alike.

In our public schools, many youth have personal issues that Christian fellowship could serve as a means by which many of their problems may be resolved. The life, the deaths, their freedom, the welfare of our children, as well as the welfare, of their families may be enhanced by them selecting Christian associate. As Christians, we must encourage Christian fellowship outside the Church walls. Secular work opportunity sponsor by Christian will encourage good work habits. It will also provide youth with not only a legal way of obtaining money. It will also provide a Christian way of obtaining money.

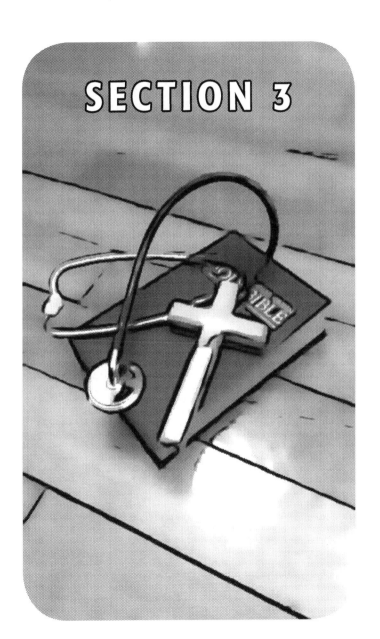

SECTION 3

What Can Christians Do?

Jesus said He expected greater things out of you as the body of Christ than He accomplished in the body. Christianity in the United States alone has a Christian population of over 224 million. The total population of the United States as of Sept. 2012 was 314, 337,197. The voting ages population 235, 404,406 of which only 91 million vote. This means that the Christian population is over 90% of the voting age population and two and a half of the voting population.

In a Democratic society, Christians can make it very uncomfortable for the devil. Christians can enhance the quality of justice in our judicial system and enhance the level of education for Christians. We can improve housing facilities for the elderly and release them of financial hardships. We can get involved in improving the safety of our communities.

There is work to do for God and country. To do this we must come to the realization of a universal faith. The church has no walls or ceilings that limit the ability to be effective and united in all endeavors. Local churches should not be comfortable with the devil dominating. No one should stand alone when they are being abused.

True Christians or one local congregation should go on mission by joining and supporting the troubled local church. We know and should expect the devil of that congregation will declare you devils and to they don't welcome your involvement.

A Christian justice center could be as small as a room in a church, or it could be as large as the Sears building in Chicago. Either way the purpose should be to release the burden of injustice on an individual or an organization or even a society. Some things that could be considered would be to retain legal representation in areas where abuse is visible.

Unjust leaders for disbarment. Promote Christian legal leadership. Encourage those you know of good report to run for public office. Openly endorse the good and do not endorse the bad. When the devil has overtaken one of the local congregations it would be in the interest of God (for a Church based injustice center) to offer assistance even as those who are on the devil's side may object. Your task would be as simple as standing up for right in a business meeting or as complicated as getting them to hold a meeting by training them with the scripture, that Jesus left them, the church assembly, to take the leadership role in enhancing His Kingdom. This is improving the world.

A secular educational program that is based on promoting Christian behavior could be as small as a room or as large as a country block. This means that this educational program would represent God in all of its endeavors. It will put fair play above winning and compassion above wealth or success. Yet, it will strive to provide an academic program which surpasses that of any country. This will be an academic program that incorporates grace, dignity and respect just as Jesus taught.

Health care facilities for the community and the congregation to release the burden of physical hardship on the young and old. Clean healthy social affairs are something that may be considered. The list goes on and on. Perhaps, some of the non-visionary leaders that steal from the church assembly feel that the assembly has too many resources, and they do not hurt anyone when they steal from the church.

Non-visionary persons should never be placed in visionary positions.

CHAPTER 6

Selecting Godly leadership

The success of any body including the Church depends on who is put in the leadership position. The first thing everybody should keep in mind is that leaders come and go. This means that it is not practical to center rules around presiding officers. It is my contention that all rules should be set up as if the devil will be in charge. (Perhaps one day he will be in charge.)

Secondly, those who are put in these godly positions would not be of bad report. A bad report would be of one who has rumors of stealing, adultery, intoxication, and no respect for truth and righteousness. There are three biblical criteria that come to my mind about selecting officers in the church. First, make sure that he or she is a Christian. Secondly, be sure that they are persons full of the Holy Ghost. And, thirdly, select someone who is among those who will be led.

Non-Christians are of the world and speak the language of the world and the world listens. He that are not of God do not hear Christians. A successful professional of the world cannot be a successful Christian leader unless he or she is a Christian. A Christian, when faced with issues, will ask himself and the congregation, "What would Christ do?" All objectives of Christian leaders are geared towards kingdom building. They always keep in mind that behaviors that turn members away from Christ is contrary to the will of God. A Christian leader should be of the mind that as a leader, he is a servant of God and the local church of which he affiliated is only a part.

A good leader is always mindful of the fact that accountability and credibility is not only the responsibility of the church, but also is the requirement of all members as good stewards of the church.

A good leader should be full of the Holy Ghost. This, to many, may appear as an impossible endeavor. How can one tell, who is full of the Holy Ghost? Those who are full of the Holy Ghost are those who keep God's commandments. The Ten Commandments is an obvious way of observing who is full of the Holy Ghost. Be aware that devils are always prepared to challenge when the Ten Commandment are used as the criteria for anything. Some of his arguments will be, "How can you judge me? How do you know I haven't changed? Everybody does it."

My advice would be if you see this behavior before selecting, don't buy it. If you see it after selection, get rid of it. The greatest element of any organization, including the church, is unity.

Adultery divides, stealing divides, bearing false witness divides, coveting divides, killing divides... the unity of the church should not be sacrificed for the favor a sinner's actions.

Identifying the ungodly Leaders

What is an ungodly leader? An ungodly leader is one who feels that the laws of God are not a reliable source to fashion one's life. They have no faith in God or the Biblical plain of salvation. They believe that there are times when God's laws are self-destructive. Therefore they should not be taught in an absolute fashion. They would say, "Do not teach, 'thou shall not lie' because lies are a good defense in life situations." They would say, "Do not teach, 'thou should not fornicate' or commit adultery because it might negatively affect their manhood," or their relationship with females." Godly persons live according to the will of God, until they find out that God is right. Sinners live their lives the way they think is right until they find out that they are wrong.

More and more, today's churches are finding themselves dealing with ungodly leaders. Ungodly leaders are adversaries of God. Their purpose and objectives are contrary to the purpose and objectives of God. The purpose and objectives may vary among ungodly leaders. Sex, authoritative, prestige, power and wealth are the five basic reasons why ungodly persons seek these positions. There are attributes that are common among ungodly leaders. They are cold blooded people. They will throw a brick and it hurts. They are masters of disguise. They have the beguiling ability to appear as a Christian. Basically, they are deceitful.

An ungodly leader is not like a godly leader. A godly leader will never ask you to go contrary to God's will to accomplish His objective, nor will he advise you to do so in other situations. If your leader doesn't have the wisdom to accomplish objectives without violating God's laws, more than likely, he is not of God. A godly leader believes and trusts in the word of God to the point of expecting trouble when he goes contrary to God's will. This is the fear of a godly man. That makes men wise.

God is love. In the word of God, the scripture tells us to love one another. Any action taken by your leader that lacks love, lacks God. In like manner, any leader that commits adultery, lies, steals, covets or kills, does not believe in the salvation of the Lord. He endangers his salvation. And, if he successfully encourages you to do the same, he also endangers your salvation. This is why ungodly leaders must be removed from godly positions. He becomes a "soul winner for Satan" in the congregation.

Ungodly leaders misrepresent the word of God and fear those who preach the gospel pure and simple. They are very protective of who speaks to those he leads. They expect you to accept their interpretation of God's word, unchallenged. Often, ungodly leaders resort to, "I am right because, as your pastor I have been blessed with special insight ability. I am an educated professional minister. I expect for you to accept what I say as being Godly, and accept the words of those I allow to speak to you."

The state of affairs of a church is a sure sign of the presence of an ungodly leader. Some of those signs are the lack of ministries, always repairing, not buying when needed, one or less employees, equipment that doesn't work, cancelled programs, the same people who distributes the money also distributes everything else.

Money is collected every other year for the same things.

The psychology of an ungodly leader is the same as any other con or cheater. It is the same because they are the same. They must convince you to trust them. The people must trust them because everybody else is said to be a thief and they are "the savior of the church." A church con understands one or two things about a good man. First, a good man does not wish to be of bad report. So the first thing he does is to put the "good man" in the position where he may obtain a bad report at his will. For example, all of the "thieves" of the church may have had keys to the church for years. They will offer the good man a key to the building on an occasion. Two or three days later they steal something from the church, then turn to the congregation and say, "See."

Secondly, the ungodly understands that a good man does not wish to be a dividing factor for the church. This is the single most reason good people leave churches. This is the single most reason why church growth is small or not at all.

The single most threatening thing to a thief are the keeping of records. Often they appeal to the congregation with the idea that keeping records away from the congregation is in the best interest of the congregation. As a result, the congregation must trust them. Here is that phrase again, "trust them," to make all decision for the church. If there is persistence regarding seeing records, they will not only threaten to destroy the church and that person's reputation, they will actually carry out that threat.

These members, your sisters and brothers in Christ, your heavenly fathers' Children your biological families, some of whom you live with. These people who are trusted on a daily basis with equipment, stocks and bonds, payroll on their jobs, business owners who have been trusted with thousands of dollars by banks, come to their place of worship and is declared a thief by the same people, not the congregation the same people, who have done nothing with church resources for years. There are good people in your congregation do not allow thieves to convince you, that there is not.

Statements that misrepresent the Word of God

1. "I am the head of this church."

2. "If you don't like the way I do things you can leave."

3. "I am the ultimate authority in this church."

4. "I am the one who determines where you work or if you work in this church."

5. "I should be the one who should present the slate of officers to the congregation."

6. "I need to know who tithes and all offerings should be presented to me."

7. "It is unchristian to vote contrary to my will."

8. "There is no need for a member to know church business."

9. "I have the authority to determine who will remain a member in this church."

10. "Any person who asks for a financial report is a trouble maker."

Where does your leader stand? If you subtract ten points from a hundred for everything that you have heard him say from the statements above. There are statements that are made specifically of the Baptist Church that is similar to the statements above, "As Baptist, we are autonomy." That means, "I can do what I want" or "We as a church can do what we want." As Christians, we are to live by every word of God. These statements are contrary to the Ten Commandments.

There are many reasons way Christians and non-Christians serve in church positions. Some of these reasons are worse than others. The word of God exalts. The exaltation of the word attracts people. Where there are people, there is wealth, power, approval and control. Unsuccessful secular professionals view these positions as a safer and easier way to accomplish their secular objective. Identifying ungodly leaders is not a difficult task. Most church members know who they are. But, they sit back and wait for the opportunity to prosper from their evil ways. Basically, there is a common path an ungodly leader follows.

Ungodly leaders make promises that are not realized. Bold and exciting, productive programs start off with a bang and usually have the support of ninety percent of the God fearing people are forgotten half-way through the financial process. Often there is no explanation of what happened to the funds or why the programs were terminated.

Productive programs and procedures are terminated or redirected, often without explanation. The ungodly leaders come into the church and remove persons who are serving well and replace them with someone that he would like to test on the congregation. Most or all of the ungodly acts of these leaders are acts that violate due process. The success of these acts are expected, by the ungodly leader, are based on the ignorant and disinterestedness of those they lead.

One sign of an ungodly leader is that they love to fix what is not broken. Things that have been working well for years (even to the point where it has become an identifying attribute) of your assembly. In like manner, they will remove anything that displays the success of other brothers and sisters in Christ. They have a strong resentment for accurate records, not only financial records but also historical records, bills, accounts, and birth records.

The Golden Calf: The Most Dangerous Leader

When I consider the most dangerous of all ungodly leaders, to the Church of Christ, Exodus 32: 1-35 comes to mind. This is where Aaron took all of the possessions of the people and made for them a golden calf to worship. Ungodly leaders make of themselves to be the "Golden Calf" to be worshipped. Those who worship the golden calf today runs into the same problem as those did in Aaron's day. The golden calf has no heart or compassion for God's people or His congregation. They also risk the wrath of God. For the Bible tells us that our God is a jealous God and we must worship Him and Him alone.

Many reasons are given to a confused body as to why all the wealth should be put into the golden calf. The most famous of Aaron's day was that they needed a God that could be seen and appreciated. He must display a value above the entire mass or congregation.

Because this image, that has been selected to worship, has no power of his own to make himself shine or be wealthy, he usually asks those who worship him to bring all of the valuables of the people to be put in his hand so that he may appear worthy to be worshipped.

The powerlessness and weakness of the calf is displayed in the request. This request displays an out of touch nature with our heavenly father, for he must appeal to the people he leads for fulfillment. Often the golden calf develops an envious nature for those the Lord has blessed in his presence. This envy goes beyond material blessings. He also envies those who display the wisdom to move anything to a higher level. This envy does more than drain the people of their wealth, it staggers growth.

Jesus, His apostles or the prophets of God, showed no interest in such material possessions. All that they had went to lift the burdens of the oppressed. The missions of the Church are ignored, for the people who built the calf can also destroy it. Therefore, using resources to please the people are put before pleasing God. The direction of the church changes from a mission direction to a money direction. Once the direction changes, the scriptures are dealt with in a different fashion. All scriptures that speak of the authority of the church, the head of the church, the commandments of God and the golden rule are discouraged.

Those who read these scriptures have their mouths muffled. They discourage open fellowship and welcome dissension.

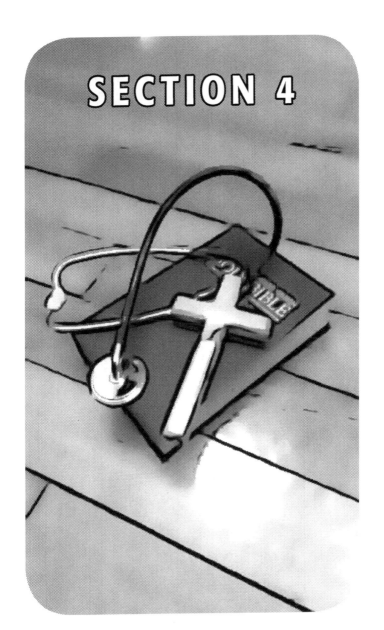

SECTION 4

Words

Listen my children and you should hear
Words of Joy and words of fear
Words that are placed upon your plate
To soothe your yearn, to meditate.
There are words that flow from heaven's door
That are mixed with potions from the devil's floor
The best of words that God may send are
spoiled by actions of common men.
To preserve the presence of your Godly notion
You must be mindful of the devils' portion
Be mindful of the words of life
It may be words of love or the devil's vice.

By John Newell

CHAPTER 7

Spiritual Warfare

What is spiritual warfare? Spiritual warfare is the battle between good and evil. It is a battle between the world of light and the world of darkness. It is a battle between God and His followers and Satan and his followers. It is the battle between right and wrong. It is a battle to retain the word of God as is, rather than changing the word of God to fit the world.

Spiritual warfare is about your level of faith in God and your level of faith in Satan. The term "good" is usually reserved for God almighty and the term "evil" is usually reserved for the devil or his angels or demons. In terms of human nature, spiritual warfare is a battle between saints and sinners. Whereas a saint is a person who has made his life available as a servant of God, a sinner is a person whose life is lived contrary to the will of God. Demons are those that encourage and advocate others in violent acts of doing wrong.

Spiritual warfare is distasteful. It is disgusting, but,

spiritual warfare is a reality. It is the reason we have Sunday school and bible study. It is an opportunity to lift Jesus the son of God up or to lift Satan and his followers. It is a time when we can ask ourselves, "How did I do?" It is an opportunity for Christian soldiers to grow in Christ.

Spiritual warfare occurs when the church declares on one hand, that the behavior of an individual or a group of individuals are contrary to the principles of God or the teaching of the gospel. And, on the other hand, when such declarations are met with strong opposition by those who refuse to conform, Christian warfare is a corrective process that is usually made worse by evil forces that are abusing God and God's people.

Why spiritual warfare? Spiritual warfare is a result of the declaration of independence that man received in the Garden of Eden. Gen 3:1-6. With knowledge of good and evil came the choice to be godly or ungodly. When we accept "good," we accept God, for God is good. When God allows us the opportunity to enhance the kingdom of heaven or to be in charge of our victories, He is allowing us the opportunity to improve our position in heaven. For forty years there were no actions of faith in the word of God by the Israelites in the wilderness.

Your soul is far more important to God than your victories. We as godly people must keep in mind, while we are waiting on God, God is waiting on us to perform the miracles that He knows we are capable of.

These are the leaders who demand control over all of the church resources, tithes, offerings, donations and even church facilities. And, what's more than that, they have the audacity to present an ironic defense for controlling everything, such as, "you should trust me because I am your leader." Jeremiah 17: 5 says, Thus, saith the Lord: Cursed be the man that trusteth in man, and maketh flesh his arm, and whose heart departeth from the Lord. How can any man be so bold as to ask the body of Christ to go contrary to the will of God.

These are the leaders that rob your local church congregation of the opportunity to do all those things that a local church congregation should be doing.

These are they, who are the reasons why local congregations are involved in token ministries (ministries that have little are no effect on local congregations, local communities, or the country). They sit in front of you with no reservation that a congregation will not demand anything of them.

As Christians we are the largest organization in the world. We have the ability to relieve our country of discrimination, unemployment, oppression, injustice and immorality. But, to do so, we must relieve God's churches of these golden calves. They are draining the blood out of the side of the body of our Lord and Savior, Jesus Christ.

When the golden calves are allowed to sit in godly positions, the door is opened for a chaotic congregation. Every sin of a church leader serves as a dividing tool in each congregation.

How many of your brothers and sisters in Christ are you are willing to sacrifice for the golden calf? Someone you know are going contrary to the will of God. When you approve wrong doing leaders in your local church congregation, you should expect the children in Christ, as well as your biological children, will follow your example by approving wrong leaders. This is what the scripture, the Bible, God's holy word says about a good leader.

Deuteronomy 32: 11-12 as an eagle stirreth up her nest, fluttereth over her young, spreadeth abroad her wings, taketh them, beareth them on her wings. The Lord alone I did lead them and there was no strange God.

The church house is not only a place of worship, it is a training ground for life eternal, as well as a basic training camp for spiritual warfare.

Types of spiritual warfare

Basically, we are able to recognize two types of spiritual warfare, direct confrontation and indirect confrontation. Each type has been at one time the preference of church members. Each type demand faith in God. The difference that generates dissention derives from the controversy between those who believe faith *without* action displays greater faith than faith *with* action.

Direct Confrontation

Direct confrontation is the method most commonly used. It usually takes the form of, "Why did you?" "How did you? "How much?" "Where is it?" "Show me." "That's not right."

The direct confrontation method not only demands accountability, but also demands the opportunity to present corrective measures. This is the method that provokes spiritual controversy inside and outside of the spiritual realms. The direct confrontation method implies that God helps those who help themselves as long as God's laws are not violated in the process. It also employs a basic concept of the Baptist faith, "the priesthood of the individual." This concept allows individual presentation of Biblical interpretation and recognizes individual revelations.

We may sight numerous direct confrontations in the Bible, Matt. 21: 12-13 and John 2:13-16. Jesus, the son of God enters the temple and challenged the sales and method of sales in the temple. In the Old Testament, Mecha, Mecharat and Debedigo received the approval and support of the son of God for a direct confrontation with the king of His day. For this process to be effective there must be a spiritually mature majority present, be it in congress or in church.

Christians that affirm this method are usually interested in church growth. They are the ones who would like to see the church move beyond its present level of enhancing the kingdom of God. In a sense they are the angels of the church. They are the ones who expose themselves to the wrath of sinners. They are the ones who present constructive ideas that are declared blasphemous by sinners. They are the ones who are called "trouble makers" by fellow members for not going along with a non-productive, ungodly program.

This method exposes wrong doing on every level. This is the least attractive method for glory seekers and thieves.

Indirect Confrontation

Indirect confrontation refers to that part of the congregation that feels that a complacent congregation is God's choice for fulfilling His mission. Their "battle cry is 'let loose and let God'."

Their premise is based on the concept that prayer, faith

and patience should charter the flow of events in Christian life. The direct concept declares that this concept must be inclusive of work in the form of what the author calls, "The Ships of Zion." Often those congregations declare those who prefer the direct confrontation approach to resolve issues of what is considered little faith. James 2:17 which tells us that faith without work is dead. This is the double-edged sword that the ungodly uses to divide and conquer.

With this concept, the ungodly amplifies the infirmities related, as well as non-related, to those of the direct approach. Needless to say, this is the selected choice of the ungodly. Here is where the ungodly unveils himself to the congregation. Here is where the ungodly assumes the authority of God, church, man and beast. Here is where a sense of God's laws, church protocol and brotherly love is not present. This group allows the ungodly the opportunity to manipulate the mindset of the congregation.

Those who have good intensions of this type of confrontation is outnumbered by the diversity of the group. This group contains those who are fearful, those who "lap the crumbs off the floor" that fall from the table of thieves, those who are waiting for the opportunity to become a part of the thieving process…those who are not truly concerned about the ministries of the church.

It is also about those who just want to be identified with whomever is in the leadership chair because the diversity of the group, as well as the "no contest philosophy" of this group, is the choice confrontational type of the ungodly.

When godly leadership is in place, either of the confrontational types prove to be a productive means for the enhancement of the kingdom of God.

The Battlefield

In any war there is a battlefields and a battle. The field of battle is often a place of greatness. The world is the field of battle for spiritual war. There is a battlefield in the internal sanctions of man that must be won before he can attempt to conquer the external ones. Spiritual battlefields are anywhere the will and principles of God is challenged. Anytime anyone stands up for what is right you have entered a spiritual field of battle. When one wrestles with the idea to repent or not, he or she has entered the field of spiritual battle. When one stands for the will of God and righteous, he or she is on the battlefield for God.

Some of the most common places of spiritual warfare are meetings in churches, schools and on jobs. There is a spiritual battle field in the judicial courts almost daily.

The church is the headquarters for Christian's warfare. It is in the church that you learn how to live and how to die.

Be not deceived, the devil is in the church and will always be there. In church of all places, the success of the devil is two-fold. He can seek to devour old and new members of God's kingdom and he can hinder the day-to-day operation of enhancing the kingdom of God.

Satan is the same in church he was when he tempted Jesus in the wilderness. He will offer to give you things that he doesn't own so that you will follow him. The devil is always seeking followers. However, the only power the devil has in church is the power that individuals give to him. This is the true tragedy of spiritual warfare in church. The devil should never have enough followers in church to make a serious difference in establishing the course of events.

Devils always seek positions in church and then demands to be followed because of their position regardless, if they are right or wrong. Many times those who do not seek truth and righteousness in their decision making process will follow these devils. No position makes a person right. No question makes a person wrong.

It is sinful leaders and not sinful members that are the number one cause of division in any church that has division. The second cause of division in the church is selfish, money-hungry individuals following "devils" anticipating personal gain and personal reward.

The success of any church lay in its ability to select those who are filled with the Holy Spirit to serve them. Many times church members vote for their friends, their family members or their clique over God, without remorse.

The Christian Soldier

A Christian soldier is one who believes in God and God's will. A Christian soldier is one who has accepted Jesus Christ as Lord of his life. Last, but not least, a Christian soldier has repented. This means that a godly sorrow for sin has changed his life. Worldly ways are no longer appealing. His mission is to live and to teach all nations to live as Jesus the Christ has commanded. As a Christian you have prioritized your life, where your love for God and God's will is always first. And, your love for your fellow man is no less than your love for yourself.

A Christian soldier's attitude should have the serenity to "accept those things that he cannot change, the courage to change those things that he can, and he should strive to obtain the wisdom to know the difference."

A Christian soldier recognizes that wisdom comes from God and is of God. Getting to know God takes precedence in his life, knowing that all things are possible through Jesus Christ our Lord.

You are the primary target of the devil in the "church house." You are the primary target outside of the church house. Your very presence is a threat. For the way you live your life lifts Jesus up and affirms the scripture.

If you are a successful Christian you are a major threat to Satan and his followers. And many times, you will be taking stands alone. Be aware, many of the fiery darts of the devil will be aimed at you.

Be not dismayed, the cause is not lost, there are 2.2 Billion adherent to the Christian faith. This faith represents a quarter to two-thirds of the world's population. It is the largest religion in the world. With the love and might of God, we shall be victorious.

Your mouth will be restrained. Your testimony will be put on the back burner. The scriptures that you will be allowed to read will become limited. Your talents will be suppressed for negotiation purposes. In private you are praised in public you are ignored. It is not in the best interest of the devil for you to be a popular figure.

The Congregation: You are the salt of the earth

A common definition of congregation may be defined as a gathering or an assembly of persons for worship and religious instruction. This definition, while it may appear to represent the purpose of a religious assembly, does not transmit the basic precept of the Church of Christ. Many of the local congregations have displayed the ability to develop worship services that are to be admired by the angels in heaven. Many local church congregations have been able to procure renowned speakers to instruct. What is not visible in this definition, as well as, in many local church congregations, is the value of serving God. Many ungodly leaders tend to reduce the act of serving God to cleaning the church house facilities.

The congregation of local churches of Christ, is an assembly called out by the assembly of Christ, which has been call out by Christ, who is head of the Church. This means that every church congregation is charged with the same charge as the Assembly of God. What we must understand is that the congregation is composed of saint and sinners, as well as, Christians of different faith levels. What we have in local congregations of churches is a diversity of souls, similar to the diversity of souls in the world.

This is a dilemma that should be illuminated for the purpose of soul winning within the congregation. This makes the church congregation the basic training ground for spiritual warfare.

Any basic training ground should have as the congregation of our local churches, have all the elements for equipping members to serve God. Many local congregations fail to recognize training opportunities within the congregation. The most valuable service you can provide to your congregation and to God is to improve the faith level of members within your congregation. As a result of members not enhancing the faith level of members around them, productivity is limited.

For any congregation to be effective, members must be taught the value and the responsibility serving God with their vote. Teaching members to have the courage to vote according to God's interpretation of right and wrong is the first true sign of spiritual growth. We serve God when we vote with truth and righteousness. Voting the way your friends would like for you to vote, voting the way you want to vote, voting the way your leaders want you to vote, voting the way Christ would have you vote, represents different faith levels of serving God.

The second most misunderstood concept about the church by many members is, in whose hand did Christ place the responsibility of the Church? The responsibility of the church was placed in the hands of the body of Christ, the Church. He did not leave the church in the hands of church leaders, rather to those who believe in him. This means that you or any other member do not have the authority to assume this authority. Christ taught when every member of the body serves and contributes just as our body does, the body serves him best.

You serve God, when you promote this principal.

The Assembly of God is charged with worshiping and instructing according to the will of God. Yet, we must not fail at the task of worshiping God, praising God or glorifying God in the most effective way…that is by serving God. There are only two choices that a congregation has to make in every situation within that congregation. It is to serve God or to serve Satan.

Congregations are lost to Satan when they do not

understand what it means to serve God. God is spirit and truth. We cannot please God unless we serve God in spirit and in truth. Our skills as a congregation must be sharpened if we are to make a significant difference in God's kingdom and in the world. As Christians we must assume the task of enhancing the kingdom of God as Christ did and in the way that Christ did. He challenged those who went contrary to the will of God.

Your responsibility as a body of Christ is first and foremost to bring new members within the fold of Christ. Any act by any member, leader or group that hinders this process is not of God.

Secondly, it is the responsibility of the church assembly to preach and teach members all that Christ taught.

Thirdly, it is the responsibility of the church assembly to protect members from the wolves of the congregation.

Fourth, it is the responsibility of the church assembly to maintain peace and harmony within the congregation.

Fifth, it is the responsibility of the church assembly to demand accountability and credibility of all leaders.

Sixth, it is the responsibility of the church assembly to insure that all tithes, offerings and donations are used to enhance the kingdom of God.

Seventh, it is the responsibility of the church assembly to develop a professional approach of retaining, maintaining, and proclaiming due process.

When any of these seven responsibilities are neglected by the body of Christ, the body of Christ suffers.

How do we serve God best? We serve Christ best when we choose "good" instead of evil. We serve God best when we choose right over wrong. We serve God best when we do not put His sheep in harm's way. We serve God best when we support God's people. This is meant when we say we must worship God in spirit and in truth. The devil is approved when we do not approve God.

When a congregation chooses to support a leader who has gone contrary to the will of God as a congregation we destroy the unity of the congregation because there will be always one Christian who will have the courage to lift Christ.

The congregation is done an injustice, as well as the leader when that does not happen. The task of the congregation is also to convert ungodly leaders, rather than allow one member to serve as a stumbling block for many.

How many sins are involved in supporting an ungodly leader? When you support him you serve His God. This violates the first commandment--serve God and only God. When an ungodly leader is served God's people are put in harm's way. When you support an ungodly leader you expose church resources. When you expose church resource you hinder the effectiveness of the body of Christ. St. John 10: 10. The thief cometh not, but for to steal, and to kill and to destroy: I am come that they might have life, and that they might have it more abundantly. St. John 10: 11 I am the good shepherd: the good shepherd giveth his life for the sheep. St. John 10: 12 But he that is a hireling, and not the shepherd, whose own the sheep are not, seeth the wolf coming, and leaveth the sheep, and fleeth: and the wolf catcheth them, and scattereth the sheep.

10: 13 The hireling fleeth, because he is an hireling and careth not for the sheep.

The first step in serving God in the way that Jesus

did is to purify your church position. This requires a congregation with a majority of them as being members of the church assembly. The Church assembly that presides in the congregation.

The four basic areas of Christ's ministry should be the four areas of concern for your assembly.

1. Christ was concerned about providing the world with the gospel, "the good news"

2. Christ was concerned about the sick

3. Christ was concerned about the widows and the elders

4. Christ was concerned about the laws that allow unfair behaviors

Jesus recognized that ignorance was and would always be a factor that would determine the rate that the gospel would be accepted. As a church it would be in keeping with the ministry of Christ to provide an educational program that would support good secular and non-secular behavior. These programs could incorporate levels of education from pre-K to college levels of study. A bolder effort of a congregation could provide physical and behavioral research.

The ministry of Jesus and healing of the sick came to be a common expectation of his ministry. This phase of Jesus' ministry may be provided by the establishment of medical centers in the churches. These medical centers should strive to provide imaging devices capable of identifying the cause of illnesses and lowering medical expense, as well as offering professional help.

Often the ministry of Christ spoke of the poor in spirit. Christ did not forget those who are of poor physical spirit. This concern was for the widows and the elders. The progressive church will not neglect providing Christian retirement homes.

Last, but not least, Christ's ministry was involved in bringing judicial injustice to the forefront of the minds of the citizens of His day. This phase of Christ's ministry may be enhanced by the establishment of justice centers in the churches. The justice center should strive to provide justice for all far beyond that which are provided by public defense establishments.

These and many other opportunities of ministry lay sleeping, waiting for the people of God to awaken them. At Jesus' departure he said, "Greater things you can do than I have done." Jesus, the Christ, wishes and expects that the work of His "preached nation," those who worship His father in heaven, shall exceed the work that He did. We have rejoiced about the works He did. Now it is time that we allow Him and His heavenly father to rejoice about the works we do.

CHAPTER 8

Weapons of Christian warfare

As a Christian you must be strong in that which you know is true. Your battle is basically defensive. Your weapons of war are those things that will protect you so that you will remain in the fight and obtain your reward of salvation. Your weapons are the truth, righteousness, the good news, faith and the word of God. Never leave your weapons. The devil will get them and claim them for his own.

There are basic tenet of your faith that should be held dear.

First, God is righteousness. There is one God of our faith. Do not be persuaded that we both can be right.

Second, seek the truth. Jesus said, "I am the truth and the light." The devil's way is the way of lies. The devil seeks safety in the lies that he tells. Christians seek safety in the truth.

A Christian must know the gospel so that he may deal with each issue as Jesus would. You are in a spiritual warfare. Lean not on your eyes and ears for understanding. Seek the spirit of God in every event. The spirit of God is found in His word. Get to know God. Knowing God comes from trusting Him. There are those who have called on the Lord our God for sixty years or more and have never trusted him. There are those who lean to their own understanding. After trusting God for so long you learn that there is security in His ways to the extent that a certain fear becomes a part of you when you go contrary to His will.

Be not deceived by those who follow the way of the devil for they do not understand you know God. They will declare your way as weak and foolish. You are to be congratulated for you have entered the realm of the spiritually wise.

Conduct yourself accordingly.

The Adversary

Your adversary as a soldier of God are those who practice the works of a dishonorable nature. Their ways are contrary to the will of God. They have a strong desire for worldly things and worldly ways. They believe that God's laws should be modified for personal use or to agree with the changing times.

They usually think too much of themselves. They are wise only in their own eyes. Their wisdom is unlike the wisdom of God. They lift up those who share their mind set. They struggle without hope to become "the spirit on the hill."

These adversaries have not conceived that going contrary to the will of God is destructive. One way or another, they will declare you as the cause of all of their problems. Vengeance is their nature. All weapons at their disposal will be aimed at someone else. Their victory lay in your unfaithfulness. Their worldly reward will be as a result of Christian soldiers going contrary to truth and righteousness. They are men and soldiers of the devil.

In Ephesians 6: 10 -20 says that after serving worldly leaders for many years as Saul, Paul became a soldier of the cross. In this chapter he expresses a concern for the safety of Christian soldiers and stated ways Christian soldiers may remain alive in the fight. He mentioned the wiles and fiery darts of the devil, which may be referred to as the weapons of the devil.

Fiery Dots of the Devil

1.	Lies	makes the unreal real in one's eye sight
1.	Slander	makes one look bad
1.	Deprivation	to keep from
1.	Discrimination	to do wrong
1.	Humiliation	to embarrass
1.	Ostracize	to put out
1.	Muzzle	keep from being heard
1.	Deceive	hide true purpose
1.	Provoke	leave faith
1.	Frighten	disarm
1.	Diffuse	divide
1.	Abuse	to make worse

The adversary will lie on you. They will slander your name and attempt to remove you from your office and from your congregation. They will officially declare you as the cause of their problem and the church problems when you speak the true about their actions.

Be not deceived, the battle is not against flesh and blood, but against principalities, against powers, against the rulers of the darkness of this world and against spiritual wickedness in high places. Yes, high places... Places as high as the senate and in our government, CEO of large corporations, deacons and preachers and pastors of churches, teachers and principals of our education system and officers of correctional systems.

The difference in spiritual warfare and non-spiritual warfare is that the enemy is not clearly defined. The battle is between the Christian soldier and the soldier of the devil. The enemy's uniform often looks just like the uniform of the Christian soldier. He is usually well versed in Christian doctrine. He often utters words of praise for his followers and those he would like others to follow.

He consistently reduces every altercation to a flesh-on-flesh basis, position-on-position basis, authority-on-authority basis, always violating church laws, properties and protocol. He demands complete trust and cooperation on every issue without any thought on your part. The proper term for this behavior is serving man. Paul reminds us in the scripture, that when we serve man we also serve that particular man's God.

Man moves from sinner to saint hood. Often this is a step process that displays levels of faith. This faith maturation level may be recognized in the life of St. Peter.

The teaching of Christ may be found in the books of the gospel in the New Testament of the Holy Bible. The purpose for which God sent His Son is the purpose Christ charged to the Church. The major purpose for Christ establishing the church, which was designed by Jesus Christ, is to enhance the heavenly kingdom of God. When we enhance the heavenly kingdom of God we enhance God's earthly kingdom. This is the seed that blossoms all of the other purposes of the Church of Christ.

Repentance, changing the hearts of man, is the foundation by which the Church purpose is realized. The degree of local church accomplishments depends on the faith level of its members. When the faith level of leadership is high, the accomplishment of church purpose is high. A sound Biblical education program of any church should be designed to enhance the faith level of its members. This does not mean that the education program should be designed to enhance tithes and offerings.

Church educational programs are supportive of Church purpose when members are encouraged to study the word of God for themselves to confirm what is taught in their assembly as being the gospel in order to grow in faith. An educational program should be designed to teach members how to serve God and how to apply what is learned. Giving tithes and offering is only one way that members can serve God. But, there is clearly distinction between "Church serving God" and "members serving God." Christ left the responsibilities of the Church in the hands of the Church Assembly of God, which is called the body of Christ.

The purpose of the Church is to complete what Christ started. Educational programs that are designed to support church purpose should include teaching the faith levels of the members, friends and the Church. Therefore, the faith level, the preaching and teaching the gospel, praising God, supporting the infirmities of others, are to relieve the burden of the oppressed.

Preaching the gospel by one person, sits high in most local congregations as a means of church members hearing the word. The word excites us. For at repentance, we come to see the good in the word and we see an opportunity for a better place in this world. The purpose of the Church goes beyond feeling good about the word. The purpose of the Church extends itself to being "good" and doing "good." The purpose of the Church is to help us grow in the spirit, filled with wisdom and grace.

In summary, the purpose of the church is to repair people not cars. The church does not have a wrecking yard for undesirables. Christ did not give up on anybody. Christ has not given up on you or me. This is what Christ told us about our God. We worship a God that has a heart. That's what makes God, God. That is the difference in our God and the God of those that worship the "Golden Calf."

A summary of the purpose of the church may be found in Matt. 28: 18-20. This is not a "let loose and let God" commandment. This is a commandment that says to the body of Christ, the Church, "Get up, stand up and get busy for the kingdom of heaven and earth have been placed in your hands."

Matt. 28:18-20 The Great commission says, "Go ye therefore into all the world, in the name of the Father the Son and the Holy Ghost."

CHAPTER 9

The Word

God is the ultimate authority in the Church

The word has come to be recognized as being the spoken word of God. Everything is because of the word. By hearing the word, man repents. By accepting the word, man receives the gift of salvation.

Jesus brings God's word to a new level, the personal presence of God in the world. The Church uses the word to improve and to be approved. Christ made it clear to Peter as a believer that he had a job to do. That job was to feed His sheep. This is an indication that Christ understood that there is work to do inside as well as outside of His Church. Christ left the task of kingdom-building in the hands of the Church. Matthew 28: 16-20 (The Great Commission) Christ made it clear to His believers that they had jobs to do. The Great commission made no distinction of country, race or gender. Nowhere in the great commission was the "let loose and let God" principal applied.

Nowhere in the scripture can it be found that God's word will one day need modifying. The word of God is the seed of life and life more abundant. The Church may be defined as a seed of God. The Church also may be defined as the body of Christ. The spirit of God is in Christ. And the spirit of God is in the church body. That makes God in you and you in God. The word and God are one.

This is a secular relationship that the Church has with God so that the wisdom of God may be recognized in the body of Christ.

Repentance awakens one to the word, as the grace of God deciphers His every word. Every Christian should be reminded to look at himself often, in terms of the Ten Commandments. Every Christian should be aware of the universal value of the first commandment and the binding nature of the second commandment, along with the wisdom of applying the golden rule. These and many other such scriptures, when taught by men of faith, has the ability to jump start those who are new in Christ. The word is received best when taught by those of good faith.

Every Church should strive to be a living example of the word. The makeup of the church should be composed according to the word. This makes God the ultimate authority of the church. When God says, "Thou shall not steal, kill, commit adultery, covet, bear false witness, or give honor to parents," and these things are not done, they are not full of the Holy Ghost. They should not be placed in any of the sacred positions of the church. The positions of the church that these people should not serve in are: pastor, deacon, deaconess, trustee, financial secretary recording secretary, head of the Christian education department, head of the youth department, head of congregational care, general church manager, moderator, head of the benevolent committee.

John 1:1 said, In the beginning was the word and the word was with God, and the word was God. The word, the scripture, the Bible... God is the ultimate authority of our lives as well as the life of the Church.

SECTION 5

CHAPTER 10

Church Structure & Constitution

Church structure may or may not be a way for a church to operate effectively. A good church structure is a scripturally based. Church structure, like a spiritual based church constitution, should never be placed in the hands of leadership to be developed. Developing church structure and constitution is the responsibility of the congregation. Often devils show their hands and heads at this time.

A devil will always be the one who points out those whom he chooses are ignorant or those who are intelligent enough to participate in the process. Pastors, deacons, Ph.D.'s are not necessarily the best choice. Those leaders must look among the congregation and locate those who are "full of the holy ghost." This means looking for those who believe in God's commandments, to the point where they have structured their lives so that others may see God's plan in their life structure.

Leadership is temporary. God's Church is forever. Often good and bad leaders encourage the church membership to develop church structure and church constitution in a manner by which they may be effected as the leader. The church should never develop or structure their constitution with the idea that one particular leader will be around forever. This is putting faith in man. Any leader that asks this of a congregation possibly has intensions that may not be honorable.

The basic way a church should be structured may be found in the Bible. God is the ultimate authority. This means no person place or things should change, alter or deviates from His will or His ways. It should be structured where God gets all the glory and the praise.

It should be structured where Jesus the Christ is known by all as the undisputed head of the church. No structure or constitution should be designed where one person (regardless of position) would have a "do or die" authority over any mission. If such a position is allowed, deacons are to serve as administrator over social and financial affairs. They are servants of the church. They work under the leadership of the congregation. The pastor is responsible for preaching scripture sound sermons.

The pastor answers to the congregation. The congregation does not answers to the pastor and his live should display a love for the church.

The congregation should be always mindful that any church document that gives one man all or most of the responsibility encourages transgress actions.

CHURCH STRUCTURE

GOD
JESUS
CONGREGATION

The **Congregational Care Committee**
serves as church manager

The chairperson of the **Congregational Care Committee** serves as the moderator

Congregational Care Committee

The Congregational Care Committee consists of every member of the congregation. This committee is the overseer of the Church. The effectiveness of this committee, as well as the Church, depends on its ability to provide the congregation with godly persons in godly positions, an educational program that teaches stewardship, discipleship, the gospel and what it means to be of "good courage." This committee must be forever mindful of those who have the tenacity to operate outside of their realm of authority.

The Congregational Care Committee will also consist of four officers and seven areas of endeavor. Each area will concentrate on the six fundamental objectives of church ministry. However, they are not limited to these specific tasks:

- Financial Secretary
- Recording Secretary

- Treasurer
- Trustee

Benevolence Ministry-Developing creative means of serving mankind.

Discipleship Ministry-The preaching, teaching, living according to the will of God, emphasis placed on what it means to be a Christian and good Christian leadership.

Stewardship Ministry-Managing church resources where church where church ministries may be enhanced by having available funds and other necessary items.

Fellowship Ministry-The coordination of members and ministries where all may experience the joy of enhancing the kingdom of God.

Recording Ministry-Provides records of past, present and anticipated future events so that the "present devils" may not cast shadows of success on persons and events from the past, present and future.

Members at Large Ministry-Provides a process by which issues are resolved. Members or committees that cannot resolve issues among themselves. They must follow the following:

Step 1. Request an intervention of a member at large who will request the presence of another member at large to resolve the issue of the church.

Step 2. The member at large and members may request that member at large committee to convene for the purpose of resolving the issue.

Step 3. The Chairperson of the Member at large committee will request the chairperson of the Congregational Care Committee to place the issue in the hands of the congregation to deal with the issue after two public announcements of the meeting.

Base Rules of Unity

No person or committee has the authority to remove or relieve any person or committee of its functions, temporary or otherwise. Nor, do any persons have the authority to dismiss or request the dismissal of another member in the church, temporary or otherwise. These actions are the responsibility of the congregation, prior to two public announcements of its actions. These statements should be stated before the congregation for the sake of new members on an ongoing basis. The Congregational Care Officers are elected by a majority vote of the congregation. No church officer may serve as an officer of the Congregational Care Committee.

Church titles may be duplicated within the congregational Care Committee for the purpose of enhancing the effectiveness of work. No individual or church committee has the authority to determine when the congregational committee should or should not convene. Any effort on the part of persons who do so merits the attention of the Congregational Care Committee. Any issues on the congregation that ten percent of the congregation feel merits attention is a reason for the Congregational Care Committee to convene.

No persons or committee has the authority to buy sell or mortgage any of the resources of the church.

An associate minister will serve in the absence of the pastor.

No income resource of disperse resource of the church shall be placed in the name of any member. All accounts savings, checking, expenditure accounts should be available to any member for review upon request form any member at large of the Congregational Care Committee. Every action of any member that effects resources of the church must be approved by the congregation as well as stated in a written certified decree and placed in the hands of historical committee for future reference. This document shall be signed by the Chairperson of Congregational Care as well as the chairperson of the stewardship committee. The members at large of the Congregational Care Committee are the eyes and ears of the congregation. There should be no business of the church that members at large do not know about. Any person who refuses to share requested information to a member at large member shall be immediately removed from office. Member at large members have the authority to sit on any meeting of the church.   Members at large have the authority to utilize communicational devises for effectiveness.

As many as ten percent of the congregation may serve as members at large members. Not any of these functions of the congregational care committee should be removed from this committee. Even though some of the functions are duplicated by other committees.

This process may be used with a constitution. And, the following two committees will serve as the developmental functional committees of the church.

Salvation Coordinator

Chair of Deaconess Moderator
Congregation Care Committee
Benevolence Committee
Stewardship Committee
Youth Committee
Communication

Pastoral Coordinator
Pastor Moderator
Worship Committee
Usher Board
Music Department
Deacons
Deaconesses

Christian Education Coordinator
Chair of Deacon Moderator
Sunday School Department
Bible Study
Transportation Department
Prayer Meeting

Church Projects

There are several ministries that the Church should offer as Christian services to the congregations. These ministries will not only be of service to the congregation, but will also create revenue and jobs.

Christian Judicial Ministry—This ministry will eliminate secular and non-secular oppression from injustice. Often Christians are caught in situations by no fault of their own, challenged by religious and non-religious systems. It will offer support professionally, financially and morally.

Medical Ministry—This ministry will provide quality physical care. It is important for a congregation to provide a certified medical center for the physical welfare of members. It would also be helpful for the church to assist in the cost of cat scans, MRIs and other imaging divides that would cause a member not to take care of themselves.

Educational Ministry—This ministry will provide certified educational programs that encourage good Christian and social behavior.

Halfway Housing Ministry—This ministry will provide housing for families who have emergency domestic situations and those who have been released from incarceration centers.

Residential Housing for the Elderly—This ministry will be helpful to members as they grow older if it may provide housing for the elderly, etc.

Social Enhancement Ministry—This ministry will provide employment, educational support and Christian social counseling.

Physical Education Programs—This ministry will provide services that promote good health through physical education and healthy eating habits.

Christian Educational Ministry—This ministry will provide ministries that would teach congregations proper Christian behavior. In addition to Bible studies the ministry will place special emphasis on discipleship, stewardship, worship and fellowship.

Benevolence Ministry—This ministry will provide church and community support.

Community Support—This ministry will provide services to the community by supporting the Metropolitan Government.